The Skip
to B

The Skip's Guide to Bowls

CHRIS MILLS

A & C Black · London

First published 1993 by
A & C Black (Publishers) Ltd
35 Bedford Row, London WC1R 4JH

ISBN 0 7136 3266 6

A CIP catalogue record for this book
is available from the British Library.

Acknowledgements
All photographs courtesy of *Bowls International.*
Illustrations by Lee Howson.

Note: throughout this book players are referred to individually as 'he'. This should, of course, be taken to mean 'he or she' where appropriate.

Typeset by Selwood Systems, Midsomer Norton
Printed and bound in Great Britain by
Butler & Tanner Ltd, Frome and London

Contents

Frances Whyte celebrates a successful shot at the 1992 Women's World Outdoor Championships in Ayr, Scotland

Introduction

YOU STAND NONCHALANTLY BEHIND THE mat, trying hard to hide a slightly smug expression under a cupped hand. You have every reason to be pleased: you hold at least five match-winning shots; the opposition's path to the jack seems well blocked by short bowls; and there are enough bowls at the back to give you some 'insurance'.

Your opponent is on the mat looking puzzled and trying to get some lucid instructions from his third. The last bowl of the match is in the opposition's hand, and after what feels like an eternity they deliver with something less than assurance. Even when the bowl races up the green, wobbling slightly, there are no alarm bells ringing in your mind. Then the bowl wicks off a very short one, travels up the green and across the head via two more fortuitous rubs, hits the jack hard against the back bowl, and the 'white' returns down the green to one of the opposition's own short bowls. People always say that a jack never comes back down the green!

The match that appeared to be won is now lost: there is no justice. This all-too familiar story illustrates the fascination and frustration that constitute the game of bowls. After such a disaster you can only grit your teeth, shake the opposition's hand and wish them well. Your thoughts may be less than charitable, but there is no point in expressing them out loud. You are the *skip*, the one who sets the example for the team; you, above all others, must be capable of absorbing the disappointment of defeat. The incident may be pushed to the back of your mind or, if you are that type of

The No. 3 has just bowled the decisive shot at the 1989 EBA Championships. The winning team, led by skip Martyn Sekjer, races to congratulate him

One of bowls' best-known skips, Andy Thomson, assesses the situation at the 1992 World Series, watched by his New Zealand opponents Ken Walker (left) and Phil Skoglund Jnr.

player, recounted for years to come over the condiments and cutlery at many a bowls tea. The conclusion of your deliberations will always be the same, however: you lost that one, even if it was to an 'outrageous fluke'.

So who would be a skip? It may seem surprising, but it is the ambition of nearly every bowler to be the skip of rink. Many think that it is the ultimate accolade for a bowler to look at the team-sheet and see his name in charge of a rink. He may or may not welcome the names of the other three players who are to accompany him over the 21 ends, but he is in charge and it will be up to him to inspire the team to victory.

How, then, does a player become the skip of rink, a position of such responsibility? This book aims to point out the characteristics that make up a bowls skip: the skills he must obtain; what he has to know; the trials and tribulations that set him aside from his fellow players. Bowling literature is not thick on the ground, and what books there are do not discuss in any depth the important aspects of skipping. It is hoped that this book will be of as much interest to beginners who are aspiring to improve their abilities with the ultimate goal of taking charge of a rink as it will be to those who have reached this exalted position but can still benefit from a further insight into what is required of them. While it will always be argued that play is the true test, the theory behind it must also be examined; a player must know not only what to do in a given situation, but also why he is being asked to do it.

It has been said that: 'Bowls is a science, the study of a lifetime, in which you may exhaust yourself but never your subject.' This is especially true of the art of skipping, as a read through this book will surely show.

Showing several rinks in action: the 1992 Women's World Outdoor Championships at Ayr Northfield

CHAPTER 1 The role of the skip

IT IS PERHAPS A LITTLE UNFORTUNATE THAT IN bowls the word *rink* is used in two contexts. First, it describes the area on which a game of bowls is played within the confines of a green; second, it is the name given to the quartet (or trio in the case of Federation bowls) of players who will use it for a team game. As the vast majority of bowls games are played in teams of four, both usages of the term will become a very important part of any bowler's vocabulary. The rink, or the quartet, must play in total harmony in order to achieve success, and there will be no place for any out-of-tune instruments. There will be a few wrong notes along the way, and the odd player will have quickly to retune, but the four must try always to follow the score on the sheet set out by the leader – the skip.

Skips have a fairly autocratic position within the team, although they must never abuse their power. A good skip will be more like a general, organising his troops by encouraging them to produce their very best, while also producing a game plan that can fool the opposition. Above all, the skip must have sound judgement when it comes to a crisis point. In dealing with their players skips will always show a sympathetic approach and an understanding of human nature. No player deliberately plays a shot badly; all must be reassured when things go wrong. However, the skip must act quickly and with diplomacy to check any slackness within the ranks: while he should not be held in awe, the skip should always be respected.

The game of bowls is a team effort, but the skip holds the key to success or failure. He holds that vital last bowl – the one that may have to avert disaster in the shape of a big-count against, or be needed to draw the winning shot. It is the skip's gift of being able to save the day when all seems lost that distinguishes him from the rest of the team. In such a case, the skip will be able to bask in the glory of success, even after being 'carried' by the other three members of the team. On the downside, however, he will invariably be blamed, no matter how well he as an individual has played, for any defeat. In short, the skip must be a true 'manager of men'.

Wales' Bryan Kingdon skips against the Scottish four at the 1991 British Isles Championships in Ebbw Vale. He is advising his player to 'come in on either side'

Changes in the game

The duties of a skip have changed little over the years, but bowls, like most sports, *is* changing – not just in the attitudes of the new modern player, but also in the way in which the game is played. A Canadian handbook written in 1902 states: 'Bowls is a quiet and philosophic amusement which depends for its success on a thorough realisation that nothing happens in it, any more than in real life, exactly according to scientific calculation.' While this may still be true in some cases, the game has since become much more competitive. As with many of today's sports, a more positive approach to bowls has overtaken the calm manner of days gone by.

The style of yesterday's masters tended to be 'draw . . . draw . . . draw'; today the more forcing shots are just as vital a part of any player's armoury as the most delicate of 'touchers'. With this new-found confidence has come one of the biggest changes in emphasis in the game. Players used to serve a long 'apprenticeship' before being allowed to move down the order of the team from *lead* (first player) to the ultimate goal of skip (fourth player). Many of today's more experienced bowlers take the view that youngsters are now pushed too quickly towards a role that demands a more stable head. The problem is that young bowlers seem to adapt so quickly to the role, often having it thrust upon them by force of circumstance, that they appear to be tailor-made for the position.

Going back forty years or more, the new player – once shown the rudiments of stance, grip and delivery – was expected to persevere at the 'front end' (lead or second player) until he acquired a level of all-round competence sufficient to enable him to play third and eventually at skip. The legendary David Bryant, who has graced the international bowling scene in the English colours for so long, will tell you how he had to play as lead for many years under the watchful eye of his father Reg. The young Bryant, however, was always experimenting and developing his techniques, which he did to such an extent that his father was eventually happy to lead while David assumed the mantle of skip.

Some players prefer to remain at lead or No. 2, never feeling happy when the responsibility of taking charge of a rink is thrust upon them. Many players will change position depending on the level of competition. The club skip may play No. 2 in his county team, while the international lead may well skip when he returns to his club. Whatever position a player assumes, **every**

one is vital to the team's success. This applies equally to pairs, triples and fours.

Singles is an entirely different matter. While you still have to play many of the same shots, you have no one relying on you except yourself, and only yourself to blame if things do not work out correctly. That is what makes the singles game so different from the others, and why some players prefer it. Perhaps they enjoy the old gladiatorial feeling – just them and the lions! Moreover, with four bowls the player has more of a chance to correct poorly delivered first or second bowls. Singles competitions do however lack the comradeship and the general sense of satisfaction provided by all-round teamwork.

Older players may well regard the changes in the game with suspicion, even regret, but there is little doubt that the general standard is higher as a result. Today's bowler is much more equipped to deal with any variation of jack position, because the 'heavier' shots ensure that the jack is moved about far more. This also requires a higher level of competence as the skip moves from draw to drive and explores the many possibilities in between. The 'controlled weight' shot became the vogue in the early '90s, although many an older bowler will tell you that this is merely the 'half-yard on' overweight draw dressed up in modern terminology. The term came from television talk, and, just as people pick up catch-phrases, what the commentators said did have an effect on the game. In the same way, the techniques of the top players was also copied to some extent. It was particularly obvious that some of the younger players had picked up the superb levels of concentration shown by such top bowlers as Australian Ian Schuback, the 1992 World Indoor Singles Champion.

Increased publicity

There is little doubt that increased publicity throughout the 1980s, due both to the large numbers of televised events and the advent of the top-selling bowls magazine *Bowls International*, did much to change not only the image of the game but also to attract younger people to the sport. In time, the younger players saw their contemporaries participate in and win major tournaments. This gave them new confidence, which brought to the game a more attacking approach and a sharpness that the older players had to counteract with experience. In many cases the age-groups joined together to form formidable units: those who resisted the changes got left behind. In some ways this helped bowls to live up to its name as a game for people of all ages.

Undoubtedly, these changes were initiated some time back with the introduction of luxury, eight-rink indoor stadia. Bowlers could now practise their art over all 12 months of the year. It could also be argued that the formation of the English Indoor Bowling Association (EIBA) as an independent body in 1971 (it had been the indoor section of the outdoor authority, the English Bowling Association (EBA), since the early 1930s) was really the light on the touchpaper of change. The first of the new stadia was erected at Thornaby, Stockton-on-Tees in Cleveland, and a new crop of 'indoors' was on the way. Since that time the EIBA has continued to flourish, with 300 affiliated clubs in 1992; this has helped to introduce new bowlers into the game, converted many 'outdoor-only' players, and provided some of those travelling over long distances to play indoors with alternatives. Those playing on the village-hall short-mats had the chance to play on a full-size green.

All this has added up to quite a different mixture, although as the sport approaches the 21st century it still retains most of its original characteristics. There are even those who would argue that in some ways its quaint nature has kept bowls in the 19th century! Whatever the changes in the game, the objective is still the same. You still have to ask yourself a few questions: 'What do I want to achieve?', 'How can I best achieve it?' and 'What is my opposing skip trying to achieve?' These will be the questions in a skip's mind when he is weighing up possibilities for the team or standing on the mat playing his own shots. It is the responsibility of the skip to decide the answers to these crucial questions. While the other players just have to follow the orders given to them, the skip has to think what shots are required to ensure victory for the team.

The spirit of bowls. From left to right: Andy Thomson, Jim O'Brien, skip David Bryant, Spenser Wilshire and Ray Hill

Learn the mechanics first

It is not possible to assume the position of skip, and make any sort of success of it, without first having a good idea of the mechanics and tactics of the game. The beginner must first learn the *draw shot* (the most satisfying shot in the game), and there is no better way to acquire this skill than to play in the lead position. However, club selectors and even 'roll-up' bowlers still have the habit of hiding a 'rabbit' (the somewhat unkindly term for a beginner) in the No. 2 position of a rink in order 'to give him time to find out something about the game' before letting him concentrate on improving his skills at lead. Much will depend, of course, on how quickly a beginner takes to his instruction and what skill he begins to show.

A front view of Will Thomas (Wales), 1992 British Isles Singles Champion, showing the 'claw' delivery. Note the concentration as he looks down the line that he wishes his bowl to take

Irene Molyneux (England) is well known for her distinctive 'elongated' follow-through. This shot is clearly 'legal'; one foot must be on or over the mat during delivery

The distinctive stance of England International Andy Thomson. The photograph shows the 'claw' grip from the side: the fingers are close together; the thumb is at the top of the bowl; and there is a marked space between the bowl and the palm of the hand

Generally, the rule of thumb is that once a player has learnt how to cast a jack, and more importantly how to draw to it, he is fit to take up a place in the team as a 'bowler'. A new player can often learn more about leading from playing and watching from the No. 2 spot! Later on he will learn just how important a role in the rink a No. 2 plays.

After an initial learning period, the newcomer must then ask himself: 'What type of bowler do I want to become?' Will he be happy to settle for the status of 'friendly player', never aspiring to more than participation in the afternoon roll-ups, or will he want to go on further by playing in club and county competitions? Although their objectives may be different, the recreational and the competitive player both want to enjoy the fresh air and hopefully the sunshine of outdoor bowling, and the close but dry atmosphere and speedier approach of the typical UK indoor stadium.

Whatever the reason for taking up the game, and whatever the motivation for staying with it, the common aim of any bowler should be to become as skilful as possible. It is difficult to enjoy playing any game badly, although in bowls it pays to persevere; while you may appear to be making no impression on the game, you will suddenly score that 'resting toucher' every player hopes for. Such odd flashes of seeming brilliance should be enough of a spur to make you try much harder to grasp the complexities of line and length with a view to achieving them more often. Everyone has their good and bad days, but what sets aside the good player from the average is **consistency**. The champion needs a much smaller percentage margin to improve his game, while the beginner has a long way to go to realise his full potential.

What then is the secret of consistently good bowling? If you knew the full answer to that you could make a good living in the game by passing it on to others. Learning the art of eye–hand co-ordination will help greatly. It involves achieving the proper stance and delivery, drawing the shot, playing to a position and driving accurately, all of which come with time.

Former World Champion Peter Belliss (New Zealand) shows a good example of the 'cradle' grip. The player has his fingers slightly apart and his thumb at the side of the bowl, which is subsequently 'palmed' out of the hand. This grip is common amongst New Zealand players, as greens in their country tend to be very fast and smooth

Cultivate a 'swing'

If all players could cultivate a good 'swing' before actually taking to the green they would find it extremely beneficial. In terms of basic mechanics, the arm is the lever by which a bowl is propelled down the green; the lever's fulcrum is at the shoulder. It works in one smoothly flowing motion without interruption. How much it goes back, and ultimately how far forward in a 'follow-through', is vitally important to the delivery of a bowl. The arm action, in co-ordination with the leg movements, forms the whole basis of a bowls delivery, and when it has been practised regularly it becomes automatic or 'grooved'. Get it right at the start and you are on the way to success: get it wrong, and many problems can arise later on.

It is not however the intention of this book to be yet another instruction manual on how you should grip a bowl, how you should stand and how ultimately deliver; there are many variations in technique and all can be effective if they work consistently for the player. The potential skip will have already responded to initial instruction, practised either on his own or by taking part in matches, absorbed the rules and etiquette of the game (*see* Chapter 7) and added the vital mental attribute of concentration. It has been said by many experts that bowls is 90% 'in the brain'. With concentration, you can convince your body to play correctly all the shots that you have rehearsed in your mind. Communications may not work out perfectly, but such a mind–body relationship should be the goal of all aspiring skips.

Concentration and consistency

When you first begin bowling you will be taught the 'mechanics' of the game, from the very simple starting-point of what bowls to use through to the best grip, stance on the mat and delivery technique. After this you will be shown the 'bread-and-butter' shot of all bowlers, the *draw*. When you are at home with this you will learn some variations on the draw, followed by the 'running' shots and finally the 'heavies'. It is highly likely that initially you will only be asked to play the draw shot, and will graduate to the others through observation and experimentation, and often through sheer luck.

1992 World Outdoor Singles Champion Tony Allcock (England) shows the 'twist' grip. In order to avoid leg contact, the hand turns as it moves the bowl back

It is still accepted practice within some bowls clubs to introduce a player to the game by handing him a set of bowls, explaining briefly that the 'bias' is on the inside (or that the 'big rings' are on the outside!) and launching him straight into a game in the hope that he picks up the rudiments sufficiently to carry on from there. Correct instruction from the start, either from a properly certified coach or from books (or preferably both), will certainly benefit the aspiring bowler and help to eradicate any bad points that can so easily creep in at the beginning.

Most bowls books, of which there are so few in comparison with other sports such as golf, cricket and football, will show you in graphic detail how to overcome the apparently simple task involved. This book, however, will assume that you are well past that stage by now and will rather concentrate on how you can put the knowledge you have gleaned and stored away in your brain's 'filing-cabinets' to its best use.

One thing that should be emphasised at this stage is the importance of thinking out all your actions. Whatever your degree of skill, and whether or not you are following instructions, you should always think about every move you make. Too often I have seen leads throw the jack down the rink in a hurried motion and then turn their back to sort out their first bowl from the pile behind them. First, casting a jack is all-important: getting the length that your skip requires is not just a matter of luck. Second, you should always know where your bowl is immediately before you are about to make your first delivery – this is part of having a tidy mind. Sweep away all other thoughts so that you are just concentrating on making your delivery. If your mind is searching for your bowl, how can you think about the main task in hand, which is to deliver your bowl correctly?

Think first of your grip and stance (get into the habit of making sure that you are holding your bowl correctly and that you are positioned properly on the mat). Make sure that you are comfortable, with no restrictions from your clothing, and that your mind is

Robbie Parrella of Australia is about to deliver his famous firing shot. This photograph shows clearly his effective backswing, and a good hand-on-knee position for balance

clear. You will now be most of the way towards bowling the shot that is required. Considering the right green and amount of weight to impart will hopefully then send your bowl on its intended course. Do not forget that if you are indoors you might need to vary your stance and delivery, and even change your bowls, to suit the much faster surfaces you will encounter.

The essential rules to observe are: take your time; think of what you are trying to do; relax so that no undue tension will destroy your control while also concentrating; and finally, be confident that you can achieve your objective. Never put down a bowl without first thinking about it.

The one complaint you will hear more than any other in bowls is that of inconsistent length. 'I just can't seem to get two bowls to finish within a yard of each other tonight.' This is usually heard more often on a faster running surface than a slow. If you want your two bowls to land in the same spot, you must make each delivery the same, just as if you have rolled them down a chute onto the green. You have to vary your length of step to achieve different lengths, and it's only when you have managed to standardise all your movements that you will achieve anything like consistency. If all the conditions were the same each time you would achieve that consistency a lot quicker; unfortunately, in bowls they are never the same two matches running, and can even change while you are playing!

As any player builds up his portfolio on the way to becoming a skip, he will soon begin to realise just how important the word *tactics* is. Bowls is a game in which tactics plays a decisive part, and the shrewd tactician will invariably make a good skip. He will test the skills of his rink against another, trying to outwit the opposing skip by not revealing his moves too obviously. There are many things that the aspiring skip will have to learn; one of the most important is the encouragement of new players. Many skips forget when they are fully experienced that they had to learn the art at some time, and avoid having beginners in

1992 World Indoor Singles Champion Ian Schuback looking relaxed as he prepares to bowl. Note, however, that his eyes are firmly fixed on the line on which he is about to bowl

their rinks like the plague. It may well be that later on they will be only too glad to receive newcomers – when other players are giving them the 'cold shoulder' because their reputations have become a little tarnished with age.

Another variation of the indoor game – Short Mat bowling

CHAPTER 2 Different types of team games and players

THE VAST MAJORITY OF GAMES IN THE UK will be played by teams of two, three or four – *pairs*, *triples* or *fours* – with the latter two being the most popular. This chapter will examine what those games entail and the role of the players in each. In some cases the line-up may appear similar, but the role of each player within the team will be different, especially with the three-bowl triples game which uses the largest numbers of bowls in any match (18).

A look at the games

Pairs

The **pairs** game is a personal favourite of many players, although it is generally only played in club or county competitions, or at 'unpopular' times at some indoors bowls clubs. Mostly it is played with four bowls per player, although the Federation code and some Association clubs do include a two-bowl pairs competition. Except where it is played at indoor clubs to a time-limit, the game is usually played up to 21 ends. The beauty of the pairs game is that both players are completely involved throughout, each taking the skip's role in deciding the build-up and eventual fate of the head. The two-bowl game, which has received so much publicity following its adoption for the World Indoor Pairs Championships, requires a great deal of drawing skill from the leads and is appreciated by Crown Green followers as a true test of bowling skill.

Those favouring the four-bowl game would argue that the use of more bowls allows a much more varied game with a wider variety of shots coming into play, therefore requiring more skill from the competitors. Whichever type of pairs game you favour, your bowling skill is truly tested both in terms of delivery and in the tactical outmanoeuvring of your opponents.

There is a variation on the pairs game which is played mainly by Australian adherents to the sport. This involves the lead of each pair playing two bowls each; the skips then play two bowls; the two original leads return to play their final two; and the skips finish the end off. It may sound a bit convoluted, but is an exceptionally interesting game as it gives players the chance to play in all the positions of a normal fours game. Its only drawback is the length of time taken up by the continual change-overs.

The pairs game provides an opportunity for two bowlers to build up an intimate playing relationship, and helps to eliminate any friction. With only two of you, it pays not to fall out! As the number of bowls has doubled from the singles game, the emphasis can switch from drawing to the firmer shots, so that two things become essential – to make sure that your advantageous position is made as difficult for your opponent to disturb as possible, and at the same time to make allowances for any disturbance that may take place. It may seem like good play to spray the jack with bowls, but a suffocated jack can prove a vulnerable target for your opponents. If you have too many bowls on the jack you have few in good positions elsewhere. Statistics show that a loose head in the pairs game, with plenty of 'ports' for bowls to go through, often provides the big-count. It also pays to avoid too many side bowls, as these can provide the ideal position for annoying wicks and resting shots. Seldom in a pairs game will you find the first scoring bowls remaining in the same position at the conclusion of the end.

Pairs has perhaps the widest ratio of attack and defence of all the games, and it is most enjoyed for its bold attacking shots – the jack trail, the yard-on take-outs, and the firm shot that can alter the balance of power at one stroke. Sit tight on a good lead and avoid rash

3

Pairs (a). John Stephenson celebrates a good shot by his skip Paul Clarke in the final of the National Pairs Championships. The dejection of opponents Brett Morley and Peter Gourding is plain to see

Pairs (b). Jersey's Maureen Allen and Mavis Le Marquand discuss tactics

adventures which allow your opponents to turn the tables. If you are on the receiving end then make sure you have plenty of back bowls so that you can go for a conversion jack-trail or forcing shot.

In pairs, the overriding principle in setting up a head is to build the best position to favour your shots, simultaneously forcing your opponents into playing the shots that they like least. It is therefore essential that you quickly discover what they are aiming at, so that you can switch your efforts if necessary. The leads will know that after their four bowls they must go to the head confident that they have carried out instructions and that the skip has shot(s) in hand with security at the back. The pairs game will therefore involve a fair degree of consultation, mutual confidence and a shared knowledge of the game. The two participants must be happy with each other's play and confident in each other's ability. It is not necessary for them to get on with each other off the rink, but they certainly must when they step on to the green.

Selecting the ideal pair is not easy: sometimes two skips can get on well together; sometimes, although not so frequently, two good leads can form a successful duo. Some husbands and wives will be able to play together successfully, and some will not. While it is better not to have two good singles players together, it can work well. It is important to remember that the most successful partnerships have evolved as a result of hard work over a long period of time. The players have had to establish their compatibility and must support each other in the choice of shots. It has been known for a good partnership to evolve from the more experienced player taking the lead position and allowing the younger, less experienced player to go skip. The lead's advice can be invaluable to a colleague, while a good skip should be able to play all the shots required by a pairs lead.

Triples

The game of **triples** may seem to be a relatively new institution, introduced as it was to the Association

Triples. The EWBA National Championships at Leamington Spa

code at county and national level in 1945, but it formed the basis of the Federation code long before that (*see* Chapter 7). Although both codes have three players per team, the Association game is usually played to three bowls per player and 18 ends, whereas the Federation game is played with two bowls to 21 ends. However, both codes can vary between two and three bowls per player, and both have their merits. Those mainly used to the three-bowl game will tell you that 'having the third bowl gives you a much better chance to succeed with at least one of your bowls'. Those playing with two say that the two-bowl game is much more skilful, and that having only 12 bowls in the head makes it less cluttered.

Certainly, the three-bowl game can suffer from a surplus of bowls, and with 18 bowls per end it does make for a more drawn-out game. Some matches in national championships have been known to go on for over five hours, particularly when several 'dead' ends take place! This tends to happen less on the slower outdoor surfaces of the UK.

In the case of the Association three-bowl game the draw, while always important and particularly so to the lead, is less significant. This is because a wider variety of shots will come into play as the number of bowls played increases. Triples therefore has the advantage of producing more forceful play, especially in the concluding stages of the game. The tactics involve the leads trying to establish the better positions, with the remaining players trying either to consolidate their work or to retrieve the situation.

The skip's most important decision in the triples game is made when the situation in the head has built up against his team. He decides when force is needed in order to make a conversion or to break up the head. He may feel that the No. 2 should do this with his last bowl, rather than leave it until his own first delivery. The advantage of triples played to Association rules is that the third bowl helps with a tactical plan.

With so many bowls in the head the element of luck is frequently seen, with 'wicks' and 'follow-throughs' frustrating even the most implacable of skips. This often has an effect of building in a variety of 'insurance' shots within the head, although it is important to get good shots in close early in the end as the head will frequently be 'blocked off'.

The key man in triples is really the No. 2, who must be able to play all the shots both in attack and defence. His speciality could well be the weighted shots, which the team may need if the lead has failed to establish a good position. It does not however follow that the skip can be a lightweight, because he must be able to dominate the last exchanges. He must have no hesitation in driving when it is required, and he will need to be fairly accurate. Triples is a game where all three players must be in form, especially in the two-bowl game. Against another good triple you cannot afford to carry one of your players.

Fours

The **fours** game forms the basis on which the Association game is played, and is the most popular throughout the world and in the UK for club matches, friendly fixtures and leagues. The members of the team are as follows: lead (first player); No. 2; third; and skip (fourth player). They play with two bowls each, usually to 21 ends.

In many cases the four players are simply 'thrown together' to play in any one particular match, and it is therefore difficult for the skip to evaluate their skills. However, when players regularly bowl together and succeed in welding themselves into a unit, fours can provide the participants with a great deal of satisfaction. In a match there can also be the added satisfaction of helping the overall team to victory by securing a good win on your rink. The success of any fours team will hinge on the ability of the individual players to execute their shots skilfully and accurately, and on the way in which the four members can work together with the emphasis on compatibility and good communication. Compatibility is certainly one of the

Fours. Club players at the EBA National Championships at Beach House Park, Worthing

main ingredients for success. However, much depends too on the skip's ability to weld his team so that the members work well together despite any differences they may have off the green or in their personalities. Even if you do not like someone, you can overlook his annoying habits off the green if you respect his ability as a player.

Much has been said about having a left-handed player in a rink. A left-handed player, provided he is of the required standard, is definitely an asset to a rink in which the other players are right-handers. He seems to cast a 'spell' over some right-handed players; his line to the jack is always different, because his forehand is the right-hander's backhand and vice versa, and he usually bowls from the other side of the mat. Use your left-hander to extract every possible advantage.

A look at the players

The lead

It is well known that the **lead** in a rink places the mat and casts (delivers) the jack. Both actions can be important tactically, and should be carried out according to the instructions of the skip. Many skips allow the lead the freedom to place the mat in a position and cast the jack to a length that suits him, and will only intervene when they feel a particular tactic is required. They may then ask for a special mat position, usually one that requires taking the mat well up the green, and for the jack to be cast either at a full or a short length within the requirements laid down by the laws. Accuracy in jack-casting is something that is often neglected, but a lead who can cast a jack to any length is of much greater value than the one who just chucks it and hopes for the best.

The play of the lead is the foundation on which a good head can be built up. Once the jack is cast, his main task is to draw to it. If he is to be relatively competent at this he must be equally adept with both hands, because quite often a rink will have one hand that bowls better than the other. The lead must get used to seeing his bowls repeatedly removed from the head, but when he succeeds it can boost the team's morale tremendously.

Leads should aspire to play their first bowl dead-length, or preferably just over, and the second bowl very close to that. Outdoors, they must also be able to counteract any problems that the wind might cause. Many leads allow themselves to be put off by their opposition; they should never worry too much what the other player is doing, although it is often the case that the 'home' player will bowl the hand that suits him best. While it is generally best to bowl the hand that you feel most comfortable with, be guided by a home player and avoid sticking to a 'bad' hand just because you are determined at some stage to beat it! It is likely that it will beat you first.

The lead will learn very quickly that skips do not like *short* bowls, which may be defined as any bowl over three feet short of the jack and on the right line. The last thing you need in the early stages of a game is a bowl in the draw that is too short to be knocked up to gain any value, but directly in the way when other players come to play that hand.

For a lead, then, the target is simple – it is the jack. He must be adept at casting the jack and playing from a mat at any length up the green.

The No. 2 position

There is a general principle in bowls that new players should always be introduced to a rink in the No. 2 position. This is not a bad course to adopt for their first match or two, because they may feel a little uncomfortable with the responsibilities of lead. While this may not have too much effect in a club friendly, however, it could have devastating results in county competitions. The No. 2 is probably the most important position in a rink. He sets the pattern for the end, and his form can make or break the team.

In order to consolidate the play of the lead the No. 2 must be the master of all shots: he must be able to play the draw to any position, or deliver a weighted shot to switch the position of strength, and this often involves shots on both hands. A good strong player in position 2 can help to avoid the disasters that can overtake a rink when the lead has missed out and a weak opposition No. 2 has failed to profit from the lead's mistakes.

Finally, the No. 2 should avoid setting up situations in which bowls will form ideal resting places for opponents' shots, and playing bowls into positions that will block their third. He should never be looking to play the drive, but should always be ready to do so if the skip asks him to. In some games skips may feel that the head is building against them to such an extent that it would be better to get it opened up earlier rather than later.

The third

If the skip is looked on as 'the boss', then the **third** is his second-in-command. He should be a player who either aspires to be a skip or has played as a skip and prefers the less responsible position. He should be a naturally forceful bowler, yet be able to draw to any position if necessary; he must be able to give the skip good advice without at any time usurping his authority over the rink; and he must have confidence in the skip, believing that he will make the right decisions during the build-up of the head. In short, a good third should be an experienced player who can give appropriate advice and guidance and who can take charge of the rink in the absence of the skip.

While a good No. 3 will always be a master of the draw, he is more likely to be asked to play weighted shots. It is important therefore that he should not be over-cautious, as he will often be asked to play a firm shot that will open the way for a skip either to deliver a winning shot or to add further to those that the team already holds. When the third takes the mat there will be several bowls already in the head, so the picture will be fairly clear as to what he has to do. A skip will appreciate it if the third can play potential end-winning shots to take the pressure away from himself. The No. 3 who has the attitude that 'if he misses, the skip will get it' is not in the long run going to be a great help to the skip.

The skip

Much has been written about the qualities of a **skip**, and everyone knows that in bowls they can be very varied. A skip's strengths and weaknesses will often be seen in the results that he produces, although this need not always be the case. A player can be a great club skip, while rarely achieving anything like the same success in the tougher competitions and on the county circuit. It is also as well to remember that a fours team is, as the title suggests, made up of four

A skip gives his pairs partner clear instructions to 'come in off this bowl'

players, and if the 'front end' doesn't perform the good skip can only keep the margin of defeat down to a reasonable level. His own bowling expertise, however, can often inspire the team to perform at its very best, and make the difference between success and failure, especially when playing a better-quality rink.

Perhaps the main attribute of a skip is a good temperament – he needs one. He will have to deal with players that do not have his ability and often let him down. It must be noted in this respect that a skip cannot always choose the players in his team. It is only in county competitions that he can basically pick his rink: at other times he will be taking command of a rink comprising players he would not himself have picked. In such a case the skip's good temperament will stand him in good stead.

It is always well to consider that many club skips think it is their right to play in that position, and object to being switched to play in another position with someone else. Too much importance is placed on the skip on occasions; it is not a position that is inherited for life. One of the advantages of the Federation game is that if the skip is having a disastrous game, as we all do on occasions, you can always change the order. That is if you can get the skip to agree first!

To obtain an all-round game all players will need to play in every position, although there will always be the odd player who prefers one position only. Invariably it is a position that they can 'star' in and one in which they are happiest. Those who stick mainly to playing at lead will often also prefer the singles game, but need the other positions to be able to hone the positional and the weighted shots.

The importance of correct instructions

The main function of the skip is to direct his players to deliver shots that he thinks are the best, in that situation, for building a successful head. Instructions to the players should always be precise and leave them in no doubt of what is required. They should, by nature, be brief, but may require more explanation if the player on the mat is unsure of something. Correct instructions form a very important part of the game. Some players abhor the use of dusters or handkerchiefs to illustrate the point a skip is trying to make. There is nothing really wrong with this; signs are often clearer than words, and help to avoid the necessity for a skip to bawl his commands down the green like a regimental sergeant major. If the sign is understood, and the player's effort is successful, the skip should quickly acknowledge it. If it is not, he should always meet this with something like: 'Hard luck. You'll get it in time,' rather than with a sarcastic repost. A player often needs the skip to indicate a hidden jack: make sure that you make this perfectly clear for as long as the player requires.

Nothing is more upsetting to a player than receiving vague instructions mumbled down the green from a skip on his haunches. Every head looks different to the player on the mat.

Human nature is such that there will be skips who will communicate to their players and those who will prefer to keep their thoughts to themselves. Tactics seem to have become more and more important in the modern game, with teams holding mid-rink conferences and discussions involving all players. The odd old-fashioned skip who believes that leads should be seen and not heard, and that the number two just keeps the card in order, still exists, but many skips now aim to strengthen their team's confidence in them by explaining a shot, especially one that seems difficult to all the players. Harmony within the rink is essential at all times, and no skip wants an argument to upset the team's play.

Sometimes, the skip may make a suggestion to the opposition that will either force their hand or make them play a wasted shot. A suggestion that a 'drive' is on will often make the opposing skip put in a back bowl which, as far as the skip who made the suggestion is concerned, will then take the pressure away from the head. It only pays to let the opposition know your thoughts when it suits your purpose!

The skip is in charge of the head. If he suddenly changes his mind over a shot that a player is just about to deliver, do not get upset over the fresh instructions. The better skips will allow their players to finish the shot they first asked for, and then explain to them – either later or on the change-over – that perhaps another shot might have been better. The chances are that changing the player's shot at a late stage will only lead to a badly played bowl. Ideally, the skip will take his time when deciding a shot and then stick to his decision. Bowls is a game played one shot at a time, and each delivery can bring about a change; skips should therefore never have a 'game plan' for a particular end worked out in advance, and must be prepared for alterations to the head when they occur. A good skip will, however, have a fair idea of what the opposing skip is thinking, and of what will happen if the shot they have asked their player to execute succeeds.

One remark that is frequently passed during bowling discussions is that many skips keep the best shots for themselves, deliberately keeping one hand open so that they can 'make the big kill' and impress the gallery. I have never believed that this is so. No skip can judge what will happen to the opposition bowls, or indeed to his own team, so he will often have to play a shot that seems unnecessary or surprising early in the build-up. Besides, if the opposing skip got an inkling that a skip favoured one hand, they would make sure that their players quickly blocked it up.

A later chapter is devoted to the principles of building a head and to what to do in a variety of situations; it is safe to say that very few players view a head in the same way. Many a skip has played an eccentric shot: despite the players' amazement ('What is he coming on that hand for?'), it often succeeds!. Good skips can successfully anticipate and counter the moves of their opponents and prevent any big-counts against their team. One point that must be remembered is that the average score per end is usually two; if you are unable to score yourself, keep your opponents down to that. If a big-count does go against, then try even harder to get shots back on the next end. It never pays to ignore a big-count, but it will need more than one from the opposition to win.

All players try to do their best 99.9% of the time, but all are fallible. The reaction of a skip should always be positive and helpful, never destructive. Praise should be given when deserved and be sincere. Displeasure rarely achieves anything, although effusive praise can be tiresome. If you do make what might appear to be a slightly sarcastic remark, make sure that it is said in a humorous manner. It is important not to humiliate a player; if he can laugh at the comment with you then the point is made without anyone getting upset. Avoid stating the obvious: any player can see if he was too heavy, too narrow or too wide. Being told merely insults his intelligence! It is better to say: 'Just a touch more green, next time,' than the proverbial 'Thin as a carrot!'.

Never turn your back on a player who has just sent down a bad bowl; that is the worst possible insult that you can pay him.

The importance of the follow-through. Wendy Line shows how the eyes should be firmly fixed on the line the bowl is to take

CHAPTER 3 The shots – how and when to play them

THE ESSENCE OF THE GAME OF BOWLS IS playing the right shot at the right time, so it is essential that a player quickly acquire the knowledge of which ones he has at his disposal. It may seem to the more experienced bowler that the following descriptions are unnecessary, but every sports player needs on occasions to revert to basics and take a 'refresher' to familiarise himself once more with the many shots available. This is especially true for players who were not correctly tutored as newcomers.

The shots fall into three basic categories: the *drawing* shots, the *weighted* shots and the *heavy* shots. There are a number of variations within these groups, and a couple of 'trick' shots that can be applied, but once a bowler has all these in the locker then he has a fair armoury with which to confront his opponents. Always remember that no bowler can really be an accomplished master of the game until he has mastered its wide variety of shots, even though he may be better at some than at others.

Whatever shot you eventually decide to play, **never rush**. Observe the length from mat to jack, the distance that the mat is from the back ditch, and how far the mat is up the green. Many bowlers in a rink have been fooled by the fact that their lead has taken the mat up a little and altered the length. This correlation between mat and jack is vitally important for getting the correct weight for any shot. Your choice of shot will be determined by the skip in a team game.

World Outdoor Singles Champion Tony Allcock has his eyes fixed firmly along the line of delivery

A look at the shots

The draw shot

The basic shot in the game of bowls is the **draw shot**. Provided this shot is executed correctly and accurately it can be virtually the only shot a bowler needs.

The simplest definition of the draw shot is: ‘a bowl that is played with the right amount of bias to finish as near to its objective as possible without touching another bowl on its travel'. To reduce the most important shot in the game to such simplistic terms may seem like sacrilege, but it is important that every player know the exact nature of each shot he is required to play. It is well known that the vast majority (approximately 80%) of shots played in bowls are attempted draw shots; the others are used either to consolidate or to attack the positions created by these.

The very first thing any beginner will be taught is that the objective of bowls is to get your bowls as near to the jack as possible. Every bowler who wishes to make progress must therefore learn to play to any length of jack, or to a jack in any position on the rink. He must also be equally successful on the backhand and the forehand.

The jack is far from being a static object: it does get moved about quite frequently, and when it does you need to have that eventuality covered. A good player must therefore learn to draw to a jack in any position on the rink. It is a good practice to cast a jack up the rink and bowl to it where it lands without centring it. Too many players can bowl well to a centred jack, but find it difficult to play to a jack that has been moved towards the 'strings'. It is not however possible to cover every possibility. The jack often seems to have a mind of its own and shoots into the most unlikely spots. In most cases a jack that is struck by a bowl travelling up the green will go backwards, but it can come back down the green towards the mat when it strikes either the back of the ditch (or bank) or another bowl. Be prepared!

When a skip is faced with a situation in which the head appears well enough covered but there is a danger if the jack gets moved, he will often ask for a shot to be drawn to an objective away from the head. The dilemma facing many a skip when the jack has been moved to the 'strings' is whether or not to take the straight route, virtually up the strings or just over into the next rink, or to take the 'swinging' hand. The choice may well already be made in the sense that one hand may be too blocked. Often the straighter hand proves the best route, provided that the bowl comes back on to the rink. It will often depend on the rink conditions, and indeed on which rink is being used. Shots that can come off on rinks two to five (on a six-rink green) may be different in this situation from shots played on the end rinks. Such variables make bowls the game it is: virtually every shot is a fresh challenge.

After one bowl has been delivered along a particular line the second is easier to determine. The main difference between the forehand and backhand shot is the grounding position of the bowl. Avoid playing 'jack-high' bowls.

Quite often a skip will require a player to bowl to a certain position that may not necessarily be near the jack but will cover a position of danger – an 'insurance shot'. This is called a *positional shot.* It is usually played to a point behind the jack except when it is played as a 'guard' or 'block' shot. The positional shot is, in effect, a draw shot, and is played in exactly the same manner. The player allows the extra green or weight to get to the position required, which is often to a bowl behind the head. It may even be to an empty space, but be used as an insurance against the effects of an opponent's bowl. Here a skip will have to be very specific with the instructions. It is not sufficient simply to say: 'Give me a back bowl;' you must indicate exactly where you want the bowl to finish. In some cases this can be within an arc of a few feet, or it may be to a particular spot. In the latter case a player will have to concentrate on the exact spot where the skip wants his bowl to finish.

The *block shot* is a version of this shot designed to obstruct an opponent by finishing somewhere in front of the jack. It is used to obstruct either a 'firing' shot or the line of a drawn bowl, and can also be termed a 'guarding shot'. Played effectively this shot can be a 'killer'; played badly it is better not to have attempted it at all! Because it requires considerable accuracy it is not tried as often as it should be, yet it should be an easy shot to play – basically, the length need only be approximate and only the line is important. A bowl that is some three yards from the jack can be just as effective as the bowl that is only three feet away, provided that they are both in the opposing bowler's line. It has often been said that even if an attempted block does not end up in the intended position it can still be in a player's 'eye'. It is generally agreed that the block shot should be delivered by thirds or skips, which is fairly obvious as you must have something to protect before trying to protect it! The block is placed on a narrow line when trying to prevent the drive, and a wider when expecting a draw. When playing this type of shot a skip must be perfectly sure in his mind of what he is trying to achieve, and not expect to block effectively with just one bowl. He must bear in mind that it is much more effective on a 'narrow' hand than on a 'swinging' hand, and more difficult to play the faster the green. In the case of the drive, the shorter it is up the green the better: it has less chance of being used to 'wick' off or to be knocked up into the head.

When to play the block is another matter. Sometimes it is better to settle for a reasonable count rather than be greedy and go for another. The five 'in hand', with protection at the front and back, is often better than the attempt for six or seven which runs the risk of being smashed up by a good drive. This holds true for most of the positional shots.

Many bowlers find that the best way to defeat a guard is to change the position of their feet on the mat, giving a wider angle in order to bowl round the guard, or by tilting the bowl to defeat the bias, which is always a difficult shot because of the need for accuracy.

Another type of drawn positional bowl is the *resting shot.* This is when the player has to reach a certain shot in the head on which to rest his bowl, thereby gaining the shot for himself or providing insurance if an opponent plays to move the jack. It is in essence a drawing bowl, using a specific target and delivered on a new centre-line from the mat, with enough weight to 'rest' on the bowl without disturbing it. A shot that does disturb the bowl is called a *wresting shot.* This actually moves the bowl from its position and replaces it, and is slightly more difficult to play than the resting shot as it needs a careful calculation of the land and weight required for it to achieve its objective.

'Weighted' shots

The next series of shots come under the category of **weighted** deliveries. They are played with a varying degree of weight depending on their intended purpose. The first of these is called the *trail shot* and is certainly one of the most valuable shots in the game. It is played to move the jack to a position favoured by the skip, and is given different degrees of weight according to how far he wants it moved. Because of the risks involved if it goes wrong, the right amount of pace is vital: moving the jack two feet could be advantageous; six feet total disaster! A skip must therefore be very specific with his instructions.

The *yard-on shot* could best be described as a wresting shot with more pace, although it must be pointed out that a skip's yard is a very elastic measurement. You will often hear a skip say: give me a shot with a yard on,' and then complain when the player executes the shot taking out the wrong bowl – 'I didn't mean that hard!' The shot is used for a variety of purposes, but mainly to open up a head without smashing it. Most of the time it is used against a single bowl or to run the jack through into a better back position. It is more precise in some ways than the straightforward drive, and requires exact line and weight to bring it off. Like the trail shot it is always easier to play on slow and medium-paced greens.

The *wick* is similar, but often results from a lucky shot or from what is thought to have been a 'fluke'. When played by your own team it was well thought out; when played by the opposition it was lucky! Used constructively, however, it is a legitimate shot. It has been likened to a 'cannon' in billiards, and can be very useful when you need to play to save a big-count against you. It often comes about by using one of your opponent's bowls as it lies wide of the head. Not enough bowlers study the benefits to be gained from using bowls to deflect their own bowl into a position of strength. If the skip can see a bowl that can be moved by striking another against it, even if it is an opponent's, he is entitled to use it.

The *plant* is another legitimate shot in this category. A genuine plant is often one of the easiest ways out of difficulty, but it is amazing how often this type of shot is missed – both by the skip failing to spot it and by the player who is told to deliver it. Care must be taken over all weighted shots, especially ones which involve the opposition's bowls. When the scoreboard shows you well down, it is amazing how often you will hit the one bowl in four that happens to be your opponents'; yet they always manage to find the right one in a sea of yours!

The drive or firing shot

The final shot in any bowler's range is the *drive* or *firing shot*. Despite its bad reputation it is a very valuable last resort, especially if you are facing a big-count against you. The firing shot should not be attempted without a reasonable back position unless you can drive the jack out of bounds. It is used on occasions to remove an opponent's bowl from the head when it may be holding out a big-count for your own team. The golden rule about playing the drive shot is: 'If in doubt, don't!' A drive is the fastest controlled shot that you will play, and there is little point in just hurtling your bowl down the green unless you are confident that you can hit your objective. It is therefore best to get your pace right so that all you then have to bother about is the right line. Avoid sacrificing direction for speed, and before you send your drive down the green make sure that the mat will not slip behind you.

Mark McMahon (Hong Kong). The player's foot position is doubtful here: for a shot to be legal the foot should be on or over the mat during delivery

There are a few more variations of those shots listed above. These could be termed as 'trick' shots, such as 'cocking' a bowl in your hand (holding it at a slight angle with the top slightly outwards, so that the bias takes longer to act); this makes it stay straighter longer. This type of delivery is used so infrequently that you need not be concerned with it. Some greens, particularly outdoors, will produce subtle variations of their own, and not always to your liking. It is part of the beauty of the game that the vagaries of the green and (in the case of outdoor bowling) the weather must be taken into consideration.

Playing the shots

The one point to remember when asking a player to deliver a particular type of shot is whether or not they are capable of it. You yourself may have the confidence to play the shot, but it may be that another player is not good enough. Avoid asking him to make a delivery that is difficult for him unless there is no other option. If he looks puzzled it is probably because he prefers another shot on a different hand. A bowler who is asked to play a shot with which he is unhappy will invariably do it badly, unless luck takes a hand and success arrives via another channel. 'Well, I didn't quite see it that way!' is a remark you will hear many times on a bowls green as the objective is achieved via the back door.

A player will therefore sometimes query the shot that the skip has asked him to play. The skip at the head may see it differently from the player on the mat. Any player is entitled to ask *politely* if an alternative shot can be played – saying briefly why – but he should remember that the skip is always in charge of the rink. In most cases the skip does know what is being asked and will often give you a choice. Human nature is such that a player will subconsciously try much harder with the shot that he has 'selected' than the one the skip has declared – although a good player will put his best effort into any shot regardless of whether or not he feels that it is appropriate. Very often a visit to the head when the skip goes to the mat to play his shot reveals what he was trying to achieve.

It is as well to remember that each player's view of a head differs. A skip must take into consideration whether his player is right- or left-handed, whether he plays better on the

forehand or on the backhand, and whether he is a pure *draw bowler* or one that can also play the weighted shots.

The skip must know each of his team members and what shots they are capable of playing. This is what makes a skip's role so demanding and different. If, as is often the case, the team is playing in a friendly fixture, he may well have a rink he knows nothing about. Then his task is more difficult, as he must weld the individuals into a unit. In some cases responsibility for the success (or otherwise) of the rink can rest very heavily on the skip's shoulders. The skip's team may be an unknown quantity in representative matches, although hopefully of a reasonable standard. It must always be remembered that all players have to start somewhere: many skips just hope that it is not on their rink!

Much will depend on the attitude of the skip and how he treats his players. The best skips will welcome all players and even treat the newcomers with more enthusiasm and encouragement than he does the others. No player, even the rawest 'rookie', wants to play badly. Judge performance on experience; take into account whether the player is nervous and perhaps trying too hard to impress. Perhaps the worst players to deal with are those who have only been playing 'five minutes' but think they know it all. The old, experienced player cannot be told anything for the same reason. Their remarks can often be very distracting for the remainder of the team; they frequently criticise what the skip is doing through sheer lack of knowledge or reluctance to acknowledge that someone else is in charge this time.

Equally, you will play against some skips who have always fancied themselves as TV commentators and give a running commentary on each bowl as it comes down the green. Be patient and make it clear in the nicest possible way that when you are in possession of the mat you want a little hush. The most annoying thing about the 'commentator type' is that their judgement of where the bowl will finish up is nearly always wrong! The skip's qualities of patience and understanding will be fully tested by this opponent.

It has often been said that you can learn more from mistakes than from playing shots correctly. If you have played a shot correctly, you know that it was right; you should therefore be able to repeat the performance when required. If you play a shot badly, ask yourself why, where you went wrong and what you can do next time to correct the fault(s). This applies particularly to the most common of bowling errors, the *narrow* bowl. It has been observed that a faulty grip, a bad position on the mat and a tendency to pull the arm across the body when delivering are the most usual causes. If you know this, you can avoid the narrow bowl next time.

Always aim to improve – some common faults

All players, including the most experienced skips, should always be aiming to improve their game. Occasionally faults creep in, or the odd bowl goes wrong. It is then time to explore what can be done to correct these errors. A good skip can often pass on advice to a beginner or to a less experienced player to help them to eradicate a problem and thus become a better bowler.

If something is going wrong with a player's delivery it could be for a variety of reasons. Possible faults can arise from:

- **the way that the bowl is held;**
- **the position of the player's feet on the mat;**
- **the forward-step taken when the player delivers the bowl;**
- **the amount of backswing of the arm when bending to deliver;**
- **the movement of the bowler's hand at the moment of delivery;**
- **the follow-through.**

First, look at the way in which a player holds the bowl. Take a look at the position of the thumb and

Paul Richards of Australia

little fingers. See if he has a tendency to lose his balance on delivery, and if his forward-step is too short or too long. If any of these are the case, the player is probably causing his bowls to wobble. The remedies are fairly simple: make sure that the little finger is not creeping up the side of the bowl; make him place the non-bowling hand on the knee of the same side and adjust his step to the right length. Always remember that a bowl should be sweetly 'decanted' on to the green as close to the surface as possible, never pushed or flipped.

Many manuals will stress the importance of 'follow-through'. It is an important part of a golfer's swing; it ensures good stroke-making by a cricketer; and it helps the snooker player when cueing a shot. In the case of bowls, a rhythmic, flowing delivery that avoids any jerking or straining is what all players should aim to achieve. Some players have a tendency to lift their heads during the delivery: to counteract this, suggest that they either make a small count (say to six) after the bowl has left their hand, or follow the bowl two or three steps up the green. Having said that, players' actions vary when a bowl leaves their hand. Most will tend to look down the line that they have delivered, hoping of course that they have chosen the right one. Others will look up even before they have delivered, as if making a final check, then send the bowl on its path.

These suggestions should help the bowler to achieve the correct line for a delivery so that the bowl arrives at the target. Failure to reach the target usually means that not enough pace has been applied, while coming to rest behind may mean too long a backswing. In the case of the bowl delivered wide of the target, this is often due to a bad position of the feet on the mat.

If the skip notices any member of his team consistently showing one of these faults, he should have a quiet word with them – preferably after the game. He should point out the fault, with his suggested 'cure', as kindly as possible. He must avoid criticising the player during the match unless he can do it without too much fuss:

this will only draw attention to the player. Often, the harder a player tries to correct a fault during a game, the worse it becomes.

A few pointers

At the beginning of a game, the trial ends should not be dismissed as an irrelevance to be got over as quickly as possible. They are very important, even on one's own green. During the trial ends you will be able to find out which are the true hands. If you find that one of the hands is a little tricky, don't waste bowls trying to master it. Always play the best hand whenever you can, but if you have to play the more unreliable hand play it correctly. A good second is always acceptable to the loss of a big-count. You will find that it is better to deliver a bowl that is too wide than one that is too narrow, because a bowl that settles narrow does so with the bias away from the jack. This means that any contact with another bowl is likely to send it even further away from the jack. In the case of the bowl that finishes a foot wide with the correct length, this has a chance of moving nearer to the jack if touched as it naturally runs inwards.

If one of your players is persistently bowling short, make him deliberately bowl a heavy one – even into the ditch if necessary! It may seem like a wasted bowl, but short bowls are mostly wasted anyway; if it helps him to find a length then it has served its purpose. Remember that if you want a player to draw to a position behind the head, stand at the level of the required position and a foot or so wide. This will help your player to be wide enough without disturbing the head. I know some players don't like this method because they feel it is making them look like a beginner, but it does help in the long run.

Watch to see if your opponents seem to prefer a particular hand. If so, get your lead to drop a bowl two or three feet short on that hand. This should have the effect of making the opposition change hand, which could upset their rhythm and leave you with probably the better hand to bowl on. If your opponents have a bowl about a foot short in the draw on the 'good hand', carry on trying to draw on that hand; it is often possible to beat that bowl with a dead-length draw. Besides, your opponent has probably left the short bowl to force you on to the 'bad hand' anyway. Even if the short bowl is touched, the odds are that it will be pushed on to the jack or beyond to be moved again next time.

It is a known fact that heavy greens tend to favour the moderate player. Good players, used to faster conditions, will have to adjust their play and accept that the odds are less in their favour. If you are playing on a heavy green then tackle a full-length jack as soon as possible. When you have found this length you will be fit to tackle the other bowls.

Remember that the heavier your bowl the better. A heavy bowl will resist the efforts of lighter bowls to dislodge it, draw a shade wider than lighter bowls of the same bias, and scatter lighter bowls when driving. Some will argue that a light bowl is more likely to get knocked up from a short position and will not resist attempts to move it. Whatever your size of bowl, do not try to force a bowl that is sitting on the jack unless you are also trying to move the jack to another position. If the back position is not in your favour, just draw a second. If the jack is hidden and you are lying a couple of shots, try to avoid leaving a bowl a few inches short, or 'jack high', as such a position could give your opponents the ideal opportunity to take shot. If your opponents fail to use it but still have a bowl left, try and move it. Attempt to keep at least one of your bowls with two of your opponents' behind the jack.

Some players will improve, while others will never get any better. Bear in mind that many players do not execute their shots correctly because they are very vague about how they should be played. It is possible for one player to beat another not because he is a better player, but because he has a sounder and wider knowledge of the game. His tactics and strategy will be more effective because he has learnt from what he has read, or been taught, in the wide school of experience. He will also have discovered that in any match the most vital element of all is **concentration**.

Concentration – the key to success

It has been said many times that in sport, and indeed in many aspects of life, **concentration** is the key to success. Anyone with naturally strong powers of concentration is very fortunate, because most of us have to work very hard to acquire them. Concentration must be worked at, moulded and cultivated so that it becomes an automatic part of your game. It often explains why some top players who are jocular off the green appear so dour on it. It is also a fact that the quiet, serious person can generally concentrate better than one with a more outgoing nature. The gregarious person often feels it necessary to continue his general *bonhomie* even while he is playing. It is vital that players should not allow themselves to be distracted by any outside influences.

Sport can generally be split into two categories; 'stationary' and 'on the move', although many games are a combination of both. Bowls, like archery, darts, snooker and golf, is played from a stationary position and arguably therefore requires more concentration than a game of football in which the player is constantly on the move. A bowler's mind must always be on the job in hand. He must not be influenced by outside distractions such as players walking up and down on adjacent rinks, especially close to the strings; shadows on the green, particularly outdoors where they can be moving all the time; and movements around the 'head' which can often be very disturbing. This, combined with some clubs' habit of taking a break halfway through a match for the traditional cup of tea, or for an outdoor rain-shower, can combine to upset the concentration of all players.

The better bowlers learn the art of self-discipline, switching concentration on and off so that they can think deeply of their game when necessary. At times this can make some players appear either more severe than they really are or full of confidence even when they are in trouble. The skip who can appear quietly confident and who is full of encouragement for his team members, even when they are being well beaten, will help them to produce their best.

Training the mind is much more difficult than training your body, so learning the art of concentration is a long process. This is especially true in the sport of bowls, which does not require tremendous strength or stamina and for which the delivery pattern is relatively easy to establish. You learn by trial and error and by absorbing the knowledge passed on by more experienced players. The latter is taken on trust: nobody deliberately sets out to mislead but some bowlers do have strange ideas. You must therefore remember that bad habits can be easy to pick up, but far more difficult to discard, especially if you do not realise at the time that they are bad habits.

The end of an end during a fours between Scotland and Israel

CHAPTER 4 Knowledge of the greens

BOWLS IS ONE OF THE FEW SPORTS IN WHICH a knowledge of the surface that you play on is nearly as important as a knowledge of the game itself. Obviously you have to learn how to bowl first – the mechanics of the game – but this will be of no use if you cannot adapt to all the various surfaces that will confront you both indoors and out. The art of the game is to roll the bowl over a surface and place it in a position of your choice. Each surface is different, with perhaps the widest variety being on the outdoor greens, and so the player must be able to adapt his game accordingly. There are certain measures you can take before the game even starts which will help to put you on the right track.

In the case of the outdoor surfaces there are many factors to consider. The texture of an outdoor green can vary tremendously, and it is very difficult to assess a green by its outward appearance. Many that look good play poorly; others that look lush and attractive play sluggishly. On the day that you have a look at an away green, the strings can be in one direction and on a particular setting. When you visit the green for your match, however, they may have changed them or even be bowling in the opposite direction.

Every rink on a green bowls slightly differently, and it is highly likely that your opponents will have chosen a rink that suits them. That is one of the advantages of being the home skip. If you are playing in a competition where the rinks are drawn when you arrive, you will have to rely on your own judgement after the two trial ends as to which is best. Make the

WORTHI

Richard Corsie and Tony Allcock watch a vital measure during the 1992 World Outdoor Singles. Beach House Park in Worthing is the 'Mecca' of English Flat Green bowls

most of those early bowls to test each hand. Too many bowlers are careless on trial ends and do not take them seriously enough. Learn what you can during the trial ends, although it is as well not to take too much notice of your opponent's bowls as they may react differently from your own.

Grass greens can be well cut or not; the ground can be hard or soft, level or bumpy and have a variety of different shades. All of these can have an effect on your bowl as it travels over the surface. Remember that the areas nearest to the ditches always get more wear than the middle of green, so there will be a tendency for them to play faster. If there has been any rainfall this will make a green run slower, reducing some of the accuracy and making for 'tighter' hands. A slow-running green also offers more resistance, and a bowl will therefore come to rest more quickly. The lighter the bowl (i.e. the smaller the size, except in the case of a heavyweight bowl), the quicker it will come to rest.

As a general rule, play the hand that suits you best and remember that you are in there to beat your opponents. Players should not make things more difficult and waste bowls by trying to beat the green as well.

If the greens are fast the player must slow down his delivery. He should take more time to play his bowls, because there is a need for far more accuracy. The lead should be looking to play a shorter-length jack and to draw close to it. The next task is to concentrate on getting a good back position. 'Touchers' will be rare, so a bowl within a foot will be a good one. Opponents' bowls should be carefully avoided, because the slightest touch can move them into winning positions; the trail should only be attempted if you are sure that there is no risk of slicing the jack instead of taking it cleanly. As a general rule, bowls played on the backhand tend to hold a fast green better and are less likely to 'run away'. Try to pair bowls rather than leave a clutch of opponents' bowls in a back position without any cover; if the jack is moved it will not then give away too much. You will need to ask players to take more land anyway to counteract the fast surface, and if there is also a breeze you will need to offset this with slightly extra land if you play the safest hand, which is the wider in this situation.

Wind will always present a problem for bowlers outdoors. If the club has a flag, look at the way it is blowing – that will tell you the wind direction and you will know whether to add weight or take it off. The general rule has always been that if the wind is behind you play the forehand, and if it is facing you play the backhand. If it is blowing *across* the green then you will know whether to take a tighter or a wider line (depending on the direction), but it is best to choose the narrow hand when you can. If the wind is gusty it is sometimes best to play the narrow hand to block your opponents, but where possible stick to the wider-drawing hand. **Wind acts against the bowl when blowing at it.**

Taking the wider-drawing hand is nearly always the best solution when you are faced with a very dry green – that is, one on which you can literally hear the bowl trundling on its path. The problem here will be that the slightest tricky patch on the green will throw a bowl off its course. You will just have to live with that and hope that your team makes fewer mistakes than the opposition. A heavy bowl will ride the bumps better, but it may be put off line on a bad 'track'.

An average-paced green will give the skip the best conditions for his players. The land should not be too difficult to judge: finding the length will be more important. Get your lead to concentrate on playing longer jacks early in the game, and make sure players avoid short bowls. Concentrate on good back positions. If the greens are wet then the draw will naturally be narrower and it will pay to be up in the head. There are also greens that are slow without necessarily being wet, and again the skip must advise his team not to be short. Nothing is worse than colliding with your own short bowls on a green that takes little bias and on which bowls pull up quickly. The skip who is a competent driver will produce good results on this type of green.

One thing that many skips forget is that during some matches the light will be poor or will worsen towards the end of the game. This is the time when short bowls start creeping in. The bowler has to compensate for an increasingly heavy green due to the evening moisture, and the jack will appear nearer than it really is. In such conditions it is best to encourage players to put a yard on, otherwise they are going to finish short. Here the advantage often lies with the skip who can bowl at the head rather than to it. Many unlikely winners have crept up the scoreboards in the last couple of ends at dusk.

A poor green is one of the favourite excuses of the skip who has never lost a match because of his own poor play. 'You can't bowl on that green. David Bryant would have struggled on that cabbage patch.' There is no doubt that David Bryant learnt his art on all kinds of greens when playing county competitions: the good player is the one who can conquer the worst first. Forget the old adage 'It's the same for both players'. There is no doubt that really accurate play is only possible on good greens and that the poor green is of more assistance to the lesser skilled bowler, especially the one who plays on this type of green most of the time. However, the good skip will put this to one side and use all his diplomacy to urge his players through trying times. It is very difficult to build a good reputation on a poor green, and very easy to lose one!

What about the bowl?

Whatever the state of the surface, you will be hoping that your bowl reacts exactly the way you intended. Perhaps it would pay to have a look at the shape of a bowl and to see why it responds as it does on the various types of surface that you will confront.

First, a bowl is *not* round, nor does it have, as many non-bowlers think, weights inside it to make it take a curved path. The bias of a bowl is due to a slight flattening on one side which leaves the other slightly heavier. As a result there are two forces at work on the bowl as it rolls up the green. The first is the forward force caused when it is propelled from your hand; and the second, which begins to affect the bowl as it slows down over the final part of its journey, is the sideways force caused by the extra weight on one side. As this extra weight is, or should be, on the inside of the bowl, this naturally pulls the bowl inwards more strongly as the bowl slows down – whether you have bowled on the forehand or on the backhand. The faster a bowl is moving down the green, the greater the forward force and the slighter the 'bend' before it reaches its target.

The effect of bias on a bowl will also be determined by the state of the green. A closely cropped, hard green will offer less resistance to the bowl than one that is soft, wet or has longer grass. This will determine the speed of the green, which can vary from 9 to 10 seconds (slow), 14 to 15 seconds (average) and 20 to 21 seconds (fast). This requires further explanation, as to the uninitiated it sounds like a contradiction in terms (10 seconds slow and 20 seconds fast).

The speed (or pace) of a green is defined as the number of seconds taken by a bowl to travel from the time of delivery to the moment it comes to rest at approximately 90 feet (27.43 metres or 30 yards) from the mat line.

Therefore, if a bowl takes 10 seconds to travel 90 feet it will be because you have taken a fairly straight line, and because the bowl has slowed down very quickly due to a high resistance. If the resistance is low you will take a much wider line to the jack, and the bowl will take longer to reach its target. It is also worth remembering that the longer the bowl takes to slow down, the greater will be the sideways force (bias) working on it.

Showing the bias of a bowl. The bowl is not weighted, as many suppose, but flattened slightly on one side

What shot to play? Some important considerations

When it comes to deciding on tactics in the case of a particular head, the state of the surface can be of critical importance. Knowledge of the playing surface and of how a particular bowler or his bowls will react to it is an all-important factor determining the choice of shot. The state of the green will often be a factor in determining good or bad length. Outdoors, whatever wind there is will contribute to this, as well as any dampness caused by rain. The golden rule is: stick to the hand that gives you the most favourable result. Avoid fighting the elements!

'There is no difference between playing bowls indoors and outdoors,' top TV commentator and former England international David Rhys Jones once said, 'but what you have to contend with may well be different.' This is certainly true. Indoors, the mechanics of bowling are basically the same, although you may have to alter your delivery – a different stance; less backswing; less follow-through, etc. – and it is possible that you may play with a bowl that is a size higher and/or heavier to counteract the greater speed of the green. A little time is needed to adapt from outdoor to indoor bowling due to the latter's greater pace. Bowls will take a much wider arc to find their objective. This may be why strings are never used indoors, as bowls can often cross over into the next rink during their course. A bowler at one end may wait for a few seconds if at the other end a bowler is on the mat and about to deliver. Bowls will also be disturbed in the head to a far greater degree than on outdoor rinks, which is why the indoor jack is heavier than its outdoor counterpart. 'Dead' ends do occur more frequently indoors, but the heavier jack helps to keep the number down.

Indoor bowls is growing in popularity, and the new stadia offer conditions that are not subject to the vagaries of the weather and the unpredictability of their outdoor counterparts. They give the more skilful player a better opportunity to display his skills, and the not-so-skilful player a chance to hone his technique. However, you still need to observe the green's characteristics, because there can be 'tricks

An indoor stadium. John Bell (left) skips at the National Indoor Triples at Melton Mowbray

and runs' and changes in pace due to temperature variations. Different makes of carpet also have different running styles, with some tending to draw better than others and some being more adaptable to heavier shots. Despite the fact that indoor carpets are sheltered from the elements, they will be marginally slower at the start of play when the heaters have only just been switched on, and slightly faster when the heat has dried the rink. It is also surprising that the weather can often have an effect on the running speed of the indoor surface: a frosty day outside will tend to make it run faster.

Artificial lighting can be very different from natural outdoor light. This causes more problems at the start of the indoor season, when the bowler has to switch from playing in natural light to playing in artificial. It is less problematic in winter, when he goes from darkness into light. Judging the distance of a jack from the mat can be tricky indoors, and the humid atmosphere does have a tendency to induce tiredness. This is aggravated by having to walk up and down on a concrete base rather than on the softer grass of an outdoor rink.

CHAPTER 5 Building the head

IF YOU BELIEVE THAT THE GAME OF BOWLS IS A science as well as an art, you are well on the way to understanding what building the head involves. Before each of your players bowls you must consider what shot the opposition is going to play and what can possibly be done to forestall it. There are many points to take into account, particularly as the state of the head and therefore the choice of shot open to the player on the mat is continually changing. The overriding consideration is to secure and retain the shot(s). If you are forced on the defensive, secure the best possible position to 'save'. There are obviously other important elements, such as securing a good back position and pairing up dangerous opposition bowls, but a skip should follow the general principle of first getting shot(s) and *then* getting positions. There is no point in securing what you haven't got!

Begin with the assumption that a lead should always aim to be up to the head and avoid bowling narrow. Provided that your lead has followed this through, and not left bowls on either side of the jack to give your opponents a perfect resting target, you can continue to build on that strength. The position of the later bowls is often determined by the early bowls, so a skip will be asking his second to consolidate the position by bowling to protect the existing shot(s). If the lead has failed to get it right, the skip should ask the No. 2 to get close and draw a shot. The third will have seen the build-up of the head and will know what his task is, whether favourable or otherwise. The basic difference between the job of the No. 2 and that of the third is that, while the second makes shots, the third has to read the head and see shots as well. A skip should always help his third to decide on a specific option: if a player has two options in mind he will tend to bowl an 'in-between' shot.

An early advantage

Building the head during the first few ends is vitally important. If you can press home your advantage, particularly when you are playing at home, and get shots on the board while your opponents are still finding the green, you only have to maintain that advantage to win the match. It is fatal to slacken your efforts around the 13th/14th end when you have built up a good lead. Many teams have been known to ease up at this point, drop a big-count and suddenly find that the tide has turned against them and they are beginning to struggle. Every end is important, but remember the three critical stages: the opening ends; about two-thirds through the match; and the final three ends. One bad end can make all the difference. If there is any risk involved, remember that it is better to settle for being one or two down than to risk giving away an even bigger count. In team games the last few ends are even more crucial, especially if the game has been close. The 'risky' shots that were taken and applauded in the earlier ends should not then be attempted. If they are, and they fail, a seemingly impregnable lead can very soon be wiped out.

The opponents, whose morale had probably been sagging, are all of a sudden cock-a-hoop and slotting shots home with alarming accuracy. They will almost certainly win the game – and whose fault will it be? Yours, the skip's. Many skips believe when they are ten shots up at ten ends that by the 21st they will be more than 20 shots to the good; this is when they take silly risks. Often, the fact that you have a good lead at the halfway mark merely means that the opposition has not yet quite settled down. Any rink that contains reasonable players will hit form at some stage during the match, and when this happens its confidence will increase. In Federation bowling you have the added consideration that the rink can change

LWIC

Building the head at the 1992 World Championships at Worthing. From left to right: Andy Thomson, Roy Cutts, Angus Blair, Graham Robertson and John Bell. They are watched by Wynne Richards, reserve for the England team over the whole tournament

A tight head, and therefore a close contest. Eight bowls cover the jack

its members about. Sometimes this is effective, and sometimes not, but it is always worth a try. It is also very important in a team game to take a quick look at the scoreboards to see how your fellow team members are progressing. If there are points at stake for winning the match, make sure that you can cover a rink that is losing. If you are losing, try to cut down your deficit enough for the others to secure the match points. While it is important to concentrate on your own game, do not forget to check on the others. Too many skips just make sure that their own rink wins, taking the attitude that it does not really matter if the opposition gets a few shots during the final ends because they are well ahead. Many a match has been lost through carelessness such as this.

The message is clear. In bowls, you can never give up: the game is not over until the last bowl has been played. A close defeat on your rink can secure an overall victory for your team.

The importance of experience – shot selection

A skip's wide experience should be evident right from the start of any match. He will quickly assess the pace and texture of the green and any possible external influences (particularly outdoors). He will pick up the 'good' or 'bad' hands from the trial ends. The skip knows that the first head of the game is vital, and will help the team to settle down as quickly as possible. He must decide what shot is to be played, always asking four important questions.

- **What do I gain?**
- **What could I lose?**
- **Can it go against me?**
- **Is it the right time to play this shot?**

Shot selection is never easy and there are many possible repercussions. Look at what can happen if a bowl is overweight or on the wrong line. Will it take out your shot bowl? Will it bump up an opponent's short bowl in for shot? If it seems that at best it will only achieve one more shot, and at worst it could easily lose five, then the percentages are really against you and you must think again. If, however, there is a chance that you could go from one to two down, but there is an equal chance of picking up a five, then there is every reason to play the shot you have in mind. Always remember that, unless the score positively demands it, it is better not to disturb a head until you have made the position as secure as possible.

When shots are against there is a tendency for skips or thirds to point this out and add: 'Whatever you do, don't be short.' The player is then likely to drop two yards short or whistle past the head. There is no need to state the blindingly obvious. If your team is four/five down, you must draw to save; this means you cannot afford to be either too short or too heavy. It is all very well to be 'up', but the danger is that the player's bowl will run past everything. A simple draw would not perhaps have won shot, but would certainly have cut down the count. This can apply when your team has left you with just one bowl in the head. It may be shot, or even second, but it could also be very vulnerable to a take-out shot.

Of course the state of a game, if it is a competition, or the overall score across your team's scoreboards may also have an influence on what shot you play. The last thing you would want is to give away a big-count and cause your team to lose a vital final. For this reason, always ask yourself: 'Is now the right time to play this shot?'

A skip will quickly realise that almost everyone will think that they can play a shot better than he. 'I wouldn't have come up on that hand,' mutters the expert from his comfortable position on the bank behind the head. 'You could see he was going to hit that short bowl!' If you are ever not quite sure of the positions of the various bowls in the head, or just not happy with the information that you have received from your third, go up to the head and have a look. This can make you unpopular with the opposition, and I personally find that it can cause a bad break in concentration, but it will help to clarify the overall situation and allow you to play your shot with more confidence on returning to the mat.

As this book has stressed throughout, the skip directs the pattern of play. How he does this is very important to the all-round compatibility of his team. A good skip must possess the ability to communicate successfully with team colleagues, both visually and orally, and his instructions and gestures can sometimes make or break a team's spirit. One thing is certain: theatrical gestures impress no one. When the position of the head requires explanation, simple and direct speech and gestures are most effective; a full-blown lecture may only succeed in confusing a player. This is particularly so indoors, where it can sometimes be even more difficult to make oneself heard.

Within reason, clear and concise instructions do much to ensure harmony on a rink. Any player, and especially one playing with a skip for the first time, will be confused if he receives unclear hand signals from the skip. When a skip asks for a certain shot, he should indicate the hand; where he wants the bowl to finish; and the risks, if any, that are involved.

After the shot he should point out very briefly what was wrong with it if it did not reach its target. 'That was the right line; you just needed two more feet of running,' will tell the player what he has to do when he is next on the mat. Clear instructions become even more necessary if the player on the mat cannot see the target, or if the jack is obscured.

A player prefers to be shown precisely what is expected of him. You must indicate the route that you wish a bowl to take and where you would like it to finish.

Tension mounts among both players and spectators during an EBA Championships

CHAPTER 6 Aspects of play

Competition – the skip's responsibilities

In every bowling club there are members who derive great joy out of friendly games that have nothing at stake. However, in today's more competitive world they seem to be decreasing in number. Those for whom competition is the zest of life are now being joined by a growing band who blend the two aspects with some success. There will always be bowlers who view every match as a mini cup final; they will often have a trophy cabinet at home which is littered with 'glittering prizes'. There is no harm in this attitude, provided it does not lead to unpleasantness, but a competitive player, and especially a competitive skip, can find a match very stressful.

The competitive skip takes the weight of the rink on his shoulders. However, while he does have to be a good all-round player, have the temperament of a saint, be a candidate for the diplomatic corps, know the rules inside-out, be a master of the art of bluffing, and have extremely broad and strong shoulders, the skip must realise that he is not indispensable.

In order to be able to cope with the pressures of his position, the skip must combine technical ability and concentration with good health. Most successful bowlers will concede that good health, and a certain degree of physical fitness, are necessary for a player to reach the top level in bowls. With all the walking up and down, a sound pair of feet and legs is necessary. There are, however, many who enjoy the game *without* being in the best of health, and some who play with quite debilitating handicaps – amputees, the partially

Elation and dejection go hand in hand in the game of bowls

paralysed and even the blind. All gain tremendous pleasure at being able to participate and to achieve relative standards. For those of a competitive nature it is as well to keep as fit as possible. Good health can often help towards your physical and mental 'keenness' and will certainly aid your concentration.

The tired player will not have a clear mind and therefore will not be able to make the right decisions or execute his shots with a full measure of confidence.

Confidence and the art of winning

Some 90% of the elements that take a player to the top are the same across all sports: attitude, courage, concentration, tactics and technical competence are just a few. The remaining 10% are concerned with the specifics which differentiate between the various games.

One of the many virtues attributed to bowls is that it teaches self-control. Every successful delivery that is made must be carefully controlled; there must be a complete absence of tension in the body, yet the mind must be completely keyed-up and alert. This dichotomy can present something of a problem, but it is something that top bowlers have to master.

In order to conquer physical tension the bowler must feel that he is in complete control of the situation and can easily accomplish the task that has been set. In other words, he must have **confidence**. Only when he is relaxed will he be able to concentrate fully on the game. The good bowler will have just the right amount of confidence; over-confidence can sometimes create problems. The over-confident bowler will let his concentration wander and this will result in a deterioration in his game. This can undermine his previous good form and help create a physical tension that will make matters worse.

I think it is quite true to say that there is a world of difference between playing bowls and playing a good game of bowls. Anyone can go out on to a green and by chance perform reasonably well; it requires an entirely different attitude actually to play a good game. Bowling is largely played with the mind, the arm and body merely forming the instruments that carry out the physical side. A clear and concise mind is therefore necessary if a bowler is to play well and win. However, it is also a fact that there is often very little to choose between the victor and the vanquished. The result of a match shows only that on the day the winner was a better player than the loser. In no way does it show that the winner is in any respect a superior human being.

A full understanding and total acceptance of this is important to your concentration when playing and competing. It can help to reduce anxieties and pressures and therefore reduce the margin between winning and losing. The state of mind of an individual is crucial when facing a big occasion. The player with inner tranquillity can put aside all thoughts of the past so that he is able to concentrate all his efforts on the moment. He will then be contesting a match with every bowl that he delivers.

Top skips are able to concentrate their minds on seeing the bowl, understand what shot they want played, and have a total awareness of all that is happening around them. The time to worry is when tiredness creeps in, because it is then that mistakes occur. Allow some time for a break in concentration, such as when a member of your team is not bowling. You can observe what is happening without becoming mentally involved. There is nothing that you can do to affect your opponent's delivery anyway, although this does not mean that you should have a chat with someone on the bank. Just take less of an intense interest. Anyway, why waste your energy concentrating on an opponent's bowl?

There will always be defeats, as in any match the margin of error can be very close. Just a few mistakes can make the difference, and then it is up to the skip to examine what it was that brought about defeat. The too-excitable player must learn to calm himself; the melancholy merchant must 'lift' himself psychologically; the confident player must keep his concentration. Each will still lose games, but hopefully will become a far more difficult opponent.

Statistics reveal that many matches are won or lost during the final ends. It has also been shown that it

In bowls there is very little room for error. England International John Bell drops a two to Ronnie Jones of Canada, who wins 21–20

is far easier to reach top form when behind than when ahead. If one team is a long way behind, the situation often becomes one of 'nothing to lose and everything to gain'. This creates a form of relaxation mixed with an increased determination, especially in the case of 'good fighters'. Keep putting in that crucial last bowl: you have what it needs to narrow the gap and pull your team back into the match.

A player must always be thinking about winning, and must refuse to be shaken by any 'rubs' of the green. It is fatal to let a little bit of bad luck disturb you: you must always believe that you can get those shots back on the next end. Do not allow your opponents any inkling that their shot disturbed you or your team. This attitude often has an unsettling affect on them.

Attitude and self-discipline

Attitude

Attitude can be an important performance-determining factor. Ask yourself why you play bowls. For you it may be simply a form of relaxation, enjoyable for its comradeship and good for the health. Perhaps you want to measure your skills against that of another human being. While these are perfectly acceptable and indeed admirable ideals, they are scarcely related to winning and losing a game. For this you must be competitive.

In serious tournament circles there are basically two types of competitors. There are those who base their game on the concept that winning is not just important – winning is everything. This leads naturally into the 'hate your opponent' approach. There are also those who get their enjoyment from simply striving to become a better player. Measure of their improvement comes mainly from beating supposedly superior players in championships, tournaments and representative matches.

The aim of the latter type of player is to improve their game through practice and skill and so to win more matches. Winning inspires this player to strive towards even better standards; losing, to define the weaknesses that allowed the opponents to win. There is no question of hating or even disliking an opponent; the opposition tends rather to be a friendly stepping-stone which can help the player to reach a higher level on the step-ladder of success. On the green this type of player will always appear friendly but competitive.

It may well be that you have no desire to hurt a friendly opponent by winning with a high score. It is important to realise that while your opponents are there to win, they also expect to see the best of your talent. Any performance that is intentionally below your best is technically an insult, even if it means that the opposition fails to score. Only if every player bowls at his best can his standard be assessed.

The ideal psychological approach to bowling consists of the mental toughness necessary for winning against a worthy opponent deserving of respect. Your will to win should be free of any 'hate' for your opponent: hate can in fact spoil performance because it tends to make a hot-headed rather than a cool competitor. It also uses mental and physical energy which is more

Stephen Rees' bowl approaches the head;

it narrowly fails to remove the shot bowl;

and the players congratulate each other in the true spirit of the game

productive if directed at your playing form. Hating to lose is acceptable, as this channels energy into playing the game and eradicates the fear of losing.

Self-discipline

There is a school of thought which holds that nothing worthwhile is ever achieved without an initial period of mental effort and growth. The body achieves what the mind has worked out, so that the more mental effort that is put in, the better the result. In bowls it is necessary to *visualise* the shot and then dispel any inhibitory negative thoughts before playing. Keep conjuring up positive pictures of yourself playing the correct shots, and as time goes on you will be able to envisage the perfect draw, the spot-on jack trail and the firing shot that hits the target.

Developing the right approach does not come overnight, however; it grows from self-discipline and intense concentration when practising both on and off the green. It should be possible to liken your play to driving a car. Most of the time a well-driven car appears to control itself, with the driver relaxed but alert enough to take action when necessary. The better you can achieve this kind of relaxed control, the more freedom you will have to concentrate totally on the game itself.

Concentrate on the next bowl that you have to play: forget what has gone before. You cannot alter a previous delivery, nor can you predict with any certainty what your opponent will do next, although you may guess at it. Worrying about a previous shot, whether it was a 'lucky wick' by your opponent or a poor shot from yourself or a member of your team, will only handicap your present and future performance. Your thoughts

must be purely positive, with all nervousness, fear and stress eliminated.

Concentration: 'active' and 'passive'

The concentration that you put into a shot can be both *active* and *passive*. When your opponent's bowl has come to rest you will be analysing what shot should be played next. Your mind will then create a mental picture of the required shot, and switch from active to passive so that with the shot in your mind's eye you can then concentrate on your imminent delivery.

It is then a case of getting yourself ready on the mat. Line up your shot; ensure that you are relaxed and not clutching your bowl; glide it away smoothly; and follow up rhythmically controlling your poise and balance. Each part of the shot can become an acquired

Even at international level, short bowls abound

skill through intelligent and consistent practice; and your personal delivery sequence, which varies from player to player, can become your passport to success. A 'grooved' delivery – one that is consistent, even if unorthodox – is an all-important part of the mechanics of bowling.

One problem from which all bowlers suffer is inconsistency in length. Generally, the faster the green, the more often a bowler finds it difficult to get two bowls finishing up together. Greens do differ in speed, both indoors and outdoors (*see* page 74). The secret lies in adapting your stride to a particular length and by raising and lowering your swing to get the correct weight. There are several successful 'wrist' bowlers who never vary their step and use their wrist to determine weight, but it is more difficult to perfect this action because of the correlation between weight and length.

Players who can judge distances have a great advantage, and those who can find both land and weight are a rarity. Accurate weight depends on how accurately you can find the land, which in turn depends on an accurate judgement of weight. To find and maintain good weight on fairly responsive greens you must use your fingers to 'feel' the bowl, weighing it constantly in your hand. On heavy greens, especially in the case of the long jacks, this sensitivity will be largely cancelled out, but on a green that is drying out with the afternoon sun you will soon feel a change and be able to improve your touch. A player must be able to spot the areas of a rink that will produce a different pace, and estimating the length of the jack from the mat is the study of a lifetime.

On heavy greens you will find yourself playing more of an attacking game. The draw will be supplemented by resting shots and 'well-up' weighted shots using free and easy actions. On more lively greens it does not pay to take too many risks; use a much wider line to the jack. Adopt a good defence, holding a decent back position and leaving enough holes for your opponent's bowls to trickle through.

In order to make these judgements the skip must be completely absorbed in the task in hand. He cannot afford to worry about failure, or his concentration will be depleted. Above all he must never allow the personality of the opponents' skip to get to him.

- **Always keep cool and have only constructive thoughts under pressure.**
- **Always appear confident and in control of the situation.**
- **Make sure that your mind only deals with the relevant facts.**
- **Always play to a plan when you are in trouble.**
- **Take your time and be positive about what shot to play.**
- **Shut out all distractions and study each head carefully.**

Motivation

Unless he uses the right words at the right time, a skip who merely shouts encouragement at his players is not going to motivate them. He must know his player: it is no good asking him, however nicely, to 'pull his finger out' if he is the type of player who will take a nose-dive if he is criticised.

Skipping is a responsible task, and the aspiring skip should think about the whole subject of motivation in a self-analytical way. A player's reaction to a given situation will have either a positive or a negative effect on his performance. He will be affected by the importance of the game; the form of his fellow players and particularly of his skip; the reputation of the opposition and its attitude to his team; 'fluke shots'; and the weather and the playing surface. The skip must consider all these factors, and assess their motivating or demotivating influence on his team.

He will very quickly realise that the study of motivation is extremely complicated, and increasingly so in team games. Players have an effect on each other; a team's performance can often be put down to one single incident that occurred during the game and the dramatic effect it had on all concerned. If the skip takes risks, he must also take into account his team's potential reactions to those risks.

Being in a wheelchair doesn't mean that you can't enjoy bowling

Believe it or not, the player on the mat is blind!

CHAPTER 7 Practice, etiquette and the rules of the game

How practice can help

It is surprising how few players practise or consult a qualified coach when they have a problem. All bowlers suffer a loss of form at some stage, and it is necessary to know what has gone wrong (whether it is mental or physical) in order to put it right. Bowlers often take each match as it comes, hoping if it goes badly that the next one will be better.

All players can improve their technique by consulting a qualified coach who will take an objective look at their delivery. The coach can then check on their stance, grip, backswing and follow-through to monitor any faults that have crept in. The role of practice is controversial, however, even amongst top players. Some will say that all players can benefit from practising shots on their own, believing that constructive training keeps them sharp and helps them to analyse shots in more relaxed conditions. However, many players have never practised in their lives and believe that playing the game is all the training they need.

Practice does allow you to improve your understanding of the game. During a match you may find yourself in a puzzling situation, and end up playing one shot while aware that another would have been better. By practising both shots in a given situation on your own you can help to avoid such dilemmas. It is true that there is no substitute for match play, but practice sessions can strengthen your weaknesses. Many a skip has wished that his lead had practised casting the jack when the 'white' goes sailing past him!

A look at the different codes

In the UK there are three main versions (codes) of the bowls game: *Association*, *Federation* and *Crown Green*. These can also be split up into indoor and outdoor, and into variations of indoor such as *Short Mat*. This book has largely followed the Association code (although reference is made to Federation variations), but does not touch on Crown Green as this is a specialist subject which should be discussed separately. The Association code, which is followed in all four home countries (England, Ireland, Scotland and Wales) and throughout the world, plays to rules set out by the World Bowls Council (WBC) – formerly the International Bowling Board (IBB), and the governing body for the game world-wide – with certain domestic changes. The Federation game is followed by some 14 counties in the north-east of the country and in East Anglia. Many clubs will only play the Association code, and a small number which will only play Federation, but most will play both codes where appropriate. The English Bowling Federation was established in the mid-1920s and is basically a two-wood game with a rink of three players (rather then four as in Association rules).

The differences in the EBF code are as follows.

- **The EBF does not recognise 'touchers'.**
- **A jack in the ditch is 'live', whilst a bowl is 'dead'.**
- **Bowls are only taken into the count within six feet from the jack.**
- **At the first end, the front edge of the mat must be six feet from the ditch, and afterwards not more than 12 feet or less than six. Objections to the mat position must be made before the first bowl is delivered.**
- **Players may change positions at the completion of any end.**
- **In rinks (three players) the lead and the No. 2 can only visit the head after either eight or 12 bowls (two-bowl or three-bowl triples) have been delivered.**
- **The jack or bowl is 'dead' when on or over the dividing string.**

- **In circumstances in which three players have to play against two, the order of play will be: lead, lead, No. 2 – repeated as necessary – followed by the skips.**

Etiquette

Bowls is perhaps one of the most sociable sports. Its very pace allows for the formation of friendships that can often endure. For many, that is what gives the game its special charm. Its unwritten code of conduct (its *etiquette*) ensures that one bowler never seeks to have an unfair advantage over another and, on the green, all players are regarded as equals. The present generation of bowlers can thank the pioneers of the game for the many 'unwritten laws' that still exist today. Proceedings still start with friendly handshakes all round and introductions that quickly put players on first-name terms.

The guiding principle for all bowlers, and particularly for beginners, is that a player should never do anything on or off the green that fails to uphold the tradition or the dignity of the game.

There will be bowlers who show impatience if you take too much time on the mat; there will be talkers, whistlers and those who hum indistinguishable melodies; and there will be all manner of players who find it impossible to keep still. There will be those who are 'experts' on greenkeeping and on bowls in general, and, at the other extreme, those who are 'totally immovable'. Bowls, as with all walks of life, is made up of every variety of the human species and you will have to deal with them all.

The best that you can do is to observe certain principles so that you, at least, are the perfect (or as near as is possible!) player.

- **Always be on time for matches and in the correct attire.**
- **Stand still and remain quiet when other players are about to deliver, and always remember that only the player on the mat is**

entitled to ask for instructions from his skip (*Possession of the Rink*).

- **Remain behind the mat or the head when it is not your turn to play.**
- **Always try to keep to the rink on which you are playing – never wander.**
- **Remember when outdoors on a sunny day that shadows can be cast.**
- **Avoid obscuring rink markers or boundary pegs.**
- **Pay attention to what is going on during the game, and especially to your skip's instructions.**
- **Always be prepared to admit a lucky shot ('fluke') and never pretend that it was intended.**
- **If you follow a bowl after delivery, keep within the rules. Try not to obscure your opponent's view of the bowl running up the green.**
- **When a skip decides on a firing shot it is as well to stand back and make sure that all players are warned so that they can avoid any bowls that 'fly about' in the head.**
- **Never openly criticise players and always try to appear to be enjoying the game, despite your misfortunes!**
- **Avoid wasting time 'arguing' about which is shot. If there is any doubt, suggest to the person asking for the shot that they get down and measure – or offer to do it yourself.**

Players often openly applaud the good shots of an opponent; this causes mixed feelings, even at international level. It takes a player with a good nature to do this genuinely, and it is really up to the individual, but no matter what you must always encourage players from your own team. When anyone has been solidly beaten by opposition that they considered to be of inferior quality, they will often say that their opponents played 'well above themselves' or 'will never play as well as that again'. No matter

On the left of the photograph Mavis Steele, the world's most capped player, watches a measurement

how good a player is, he will always meet with defeat: bowls is very much a game for the day. Remember that a player who has played at his best has only reproduced a form that he is capable of repeating.

Knowing the laws

It quickly becomes obvious if you attempt to progress with a bowling career in ignorance of the game's laws. All sports have their rules and regulations, and bowls is no exception. While we may feel that some of the laws are a little ambiguous, to say the least, nevertheless they are there and should be adhered to. Many bowlers seem to have only a rough grasp of these laws, and when it comes to a dispute often have to counsel others to arbitrate. Fortunately, in my position as editor of *Bowls International* I have had to study these laws thoroughly, and have found the answers to our 'Umpires Corner' from English Bowls Umpires Association secretary Norman Deeprose very interesting.

Some laws are more abused than others. It is a fact that very few of the laws of bowls carry any penalties.

A measurement has just taken place, as a result of which the player on the ground concedes shot to the opposition

For the most part they merely outline the way in which the game is to be played. One law that does carry a penalty is the *foot-fault* law, and it is one that causes a lot of controversy. Foot-faults occur regularly and are rarely penalised, although an umpire can warn a player and subsequently remove a bowl if the player transgresses again. Quite often a player's knowledge of the 'Possession of the Rink' rule leaves a lot to be desired. In most cases it is genuine ignorance, or forgetfulness, rather than any attempt at gamesmanship that causes them to transgress, although there are one or two who make attempts at trying to put another player off while bowling. If an opponent does this, try first to give him the benefit of the doubt. If he persists, and it becomes obvious that he knows what he is doing, then you may have no alternative but to seek a ruling from a higher authority to get it stopped.

Fortunately, this situation is rare and many bowlers will sail through life without ever having to deal with an unscrupulous opponent. From what I can gather it often happens more at club level than at county and international. Beware the player with the 'elastic' measure! Make sure that one end touches the jack and that the measure is not bent in any way. When the measure is tight, gaining just a quarter of an inch can help.

Be careful not to confuse tactics with gamesmanship. Tactics that put an opponent off his game, provided they are legal, are quite in order. The skip who asks his lead to 'take the mat up' in a bid to put his opponents off is not cheating. The skip who sends down a salvo of heavy bowls in a bid to unsettle an opposing skip is quite entitled to do so. However, the players who indulge in unnecessary movements in the head, breaking up the head before an opponent has had time to inspect the number of shots, and indulge in time-wasting tactics are flouting the laws. The line between gamesmanship and tactics is sometimes very narrow. An ill-chosen remark at an important psychological moment may be very difficult to prove or define, but be on your guard. Most bowlers would not want to get involved in an unpleasant scene.

A good skip will remain calm and composed no matter what the provocation. He should refuse to surrender to what are probably desperate measures by an opponent.

Rules and regulations made simple

Rather than print the laws of the WBC and EBF code variations, which are often couched in confusing terms, a quick look at some of the main points may be helpful.

- **The instrument of all our torture is a *bowl* not a *wood* . . . (after all, they used to play football with a pigs-bladder; we do not call the game 'pigs-bladder' now). The *jack* can be either a 'cot' or a 'kitty' (and, like your bowls, a lot more it it doesn't behave).**
- **A *green* is the whole playing area, while a *rink* is both part of a green and a group of**

four players (or three in Federation circles) comprising a team.

- ***Bowls* come in nine sizes (00–7), and indoor *jacks* are heavier than outdoor jacks (382–453 g and 227–83 g respectively).**

Starting the match

The first thing to do before the match commences is to toss a coin to see who starts. The winner has a choice: mat and jack, or give them to the opponent. There are a lot of bowlers who think that winning means you automatically go first; think about it, though. Sometimes it is better to have the last bowl. Thereafter the winner of the preceding scoring end goes first.

You are then normally allowed two *trial ends* (one each way). These are not part of the game, so your mat can be placed where you like within the rules.

On the first end you must place the mat (front edge) 6 ft from the ditch behind you. After that it must be *no less* than 6 ft (12 ft by EBF rules). It must also be no less than 76 ft (EBA) or 81 ft (EIBA) from the *front* ditch. Confused? There's more to come!

If a *jack* finishes less than 6 ft from the front ditch, it is moved back to 6 ft and must be cast (delivered) at least 75 ft (EIBA and EBF) or 70 ft (EBA) from the front edge of the mat. If it is not delivered properly then it is returned and the opposing player gets his chance to 'set' the jack. He does not however play first. If both players deliver improperly twice then it is set 6 ft from the front ditch and the player who delivered first can put the mat in a position of his choice – within the rules, of course.

Stand and deliver!

When delivering a bowl you must have one foot *on or over* the mat. If you do not, this constitutes a *foot-fault* for which a bowl can be stopped and declared 'dead'. This is a rare phenomenon, but the rule is there and according to many players should be applied more stringently.

'Dead or alive'

Bowls are either '*dead*' or '*live*'. At this stage it is necessary to introduce the famous *toucher* – well known in Association circles. Quite simply, it is a bowl that on its course touches the jack, or falls over on to the jack before the next bowl comes to rest, and remains within the confines of the rink. It can hit any number of bowls on its way to the jack. This bowl is then marked with chalk or sprayed from one of the new chalk-spray cans and it remains a '*live*' bowl until it leaves the rink. Any other bowl is a '*non-toucher*'.

A *live* bowl is one that comes to rest within the boundaries of the rink and not less than 45 ft from the front of the mat. A *dead* bowl is a non-toucher that comes to rest either in the ditch or off the rink (outside the boundaries). A bowl is not dead if it is carried up the green by a player inspecting the head, but he must be careful not to drop it! In Federation circles you are not even allowed to put it down. Note that a bowl under EBA rules is not dead until it is entirely beyond the confines of the rink, whereas under EBF rules it is declared dead if it is touching the strings.

A *jack* can be live when it is taken into the ditch by a bowl and remains within the boundaries of the rink. The bowl will either be live or dead: if the former, it will remain; if the latter it will be removed.

An *end* can be declared dead for a number of reasons, but usually when the jack has been knocked out of the rink. It can also be dead because either a bowl(s) or the jack have been interfered with. In this case a skip has four options:

- **to have the bowl (or jack) restored as near as possible to its original position;**
- **to let the disturbed bowl (or jack) remain where it finally rested;**
- **to have the bowl that disturbed the head declared dead;**
- **to call for the end to be replayed.**

Changing places

The basis of the Association game is fours, and it must be remembered that in this game the players must remain in the positions that are stated on the card. In the Federation game, which is based on triples, players can exchange places after each completed end. The duties of a four are as follows:

- **lead** – places the mat and delivers the jack;
- **second** – keeps the score on the card and scoreboard;
- **third** – measures;
- **skip** – directs and takes the rap when defeated.

The last player to play the last bowl in any end is under no obligation to do so, but he must make his intentions clear to the opposition so that a declaration of the end can take place. Once he has done this he cannot change his mind.

Scoring

Nothing could be simpler. For each of your bowls that is nearer to the jack than the nearest of your opponent's, count one shot. Remember the cardinal rule: 'If in doubt, measure out.'

CHAPTER 8 In brief

- **Ensure that all players enjoy bowling with you.**
- **Never criticise your team: give only praise and constructive advice.**
- **Discuss tactics with the whole team.**
- **Be a 'confidence booster'.**
- **Always consider what is best for the team.**
- **Always give clear and concise instructions.**
- **Always appear relaxed and be approachable at all times.**
- **Be conversant with the rules.**

Easy, isn't it!

Signing autographs for young fans is part of the top player's routine

The joy of victory. The winning team at the England/Scotland Junior International, staged for the first time in 1990

Sheer elation – a successful shot in the semi-final of the 1992 Middleton Cup

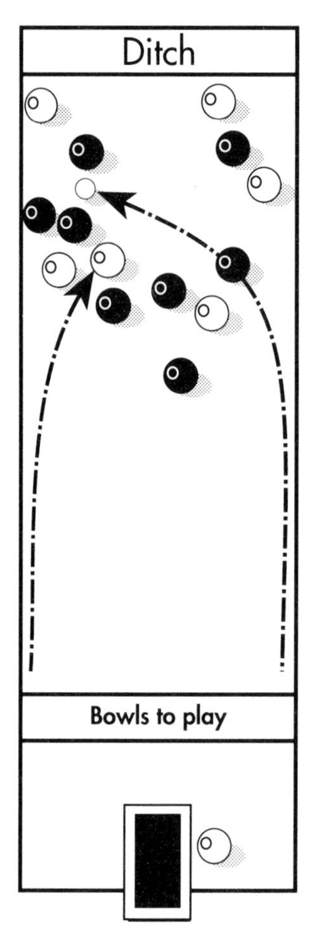

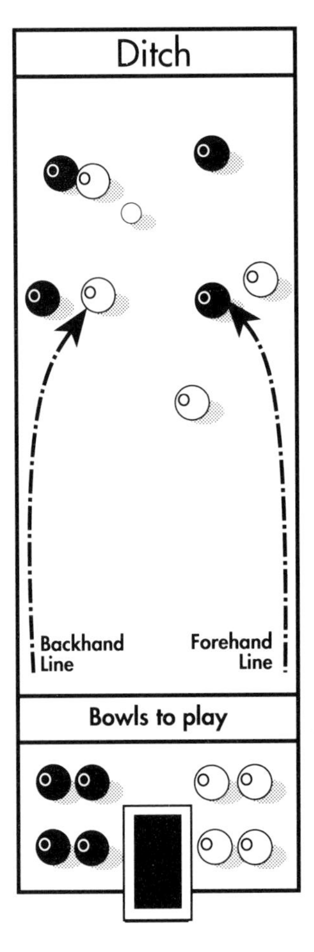

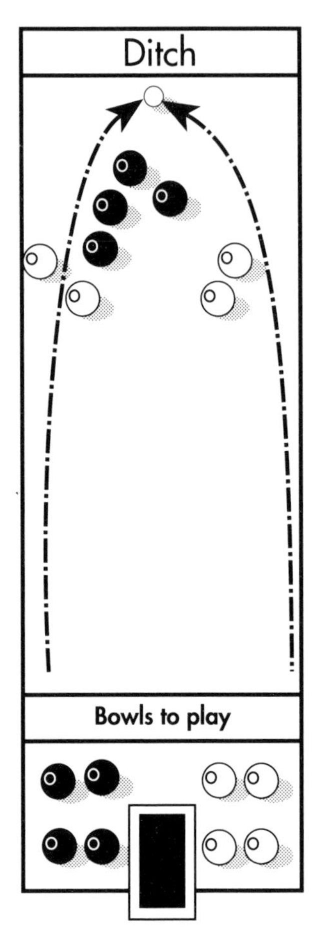

In an attempt to prevent B from scoring, W have played 'blockers' and back bowls; W skip's 1st bowl draws shot to save. B skip's last bowl trails the jack back for 3 shots. W skip has 1 to play to an off-centre, well-covered jack. *Best shot*: a backhand shot with weight to move the jack back to a more favourable position, either to cut the count or to give shot

W hold shot but B lead by 1 in the 21st end of a fours. B No. 3 is about to play his 1st bowl. A draw shot is very difficult: W have the last bowl, and a blocking bowl in the driving position partly covers the shot. *Best shot*: a forehand with about 4 ft of weight just inside the drawline, either to wick off B's short bowl and pick up the jack, or to face the shot bowl. *Prime object*: to change the head

W lead by 3 in an indoor fours. The green runs at 15 seconds and the forehand has a wider draw. W lead and W second have both played the tighter backhand and been short; W No. 3 has played the backhand well with weight, but this time wants to draw on the open forehand with his 1st bowl. *Best shot*: a forehand with weight to clear some of B's scoring bowls out of the way. In giving these instructions W skip must be diplomatic!

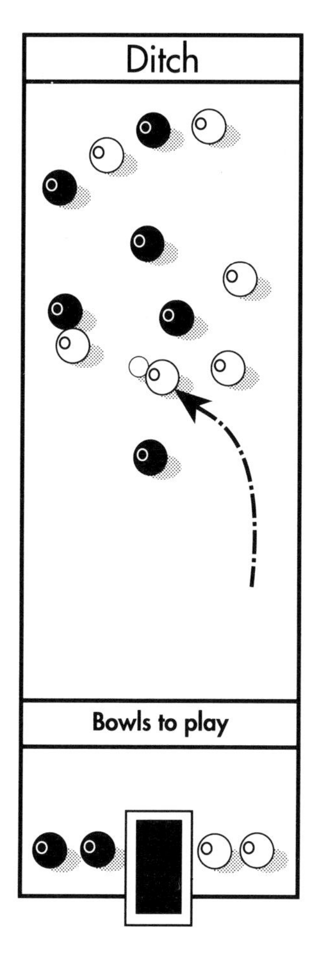

A typical draw shot with W possibly behind by 2 (although there is still the opportunity for B to trail on the backhand)

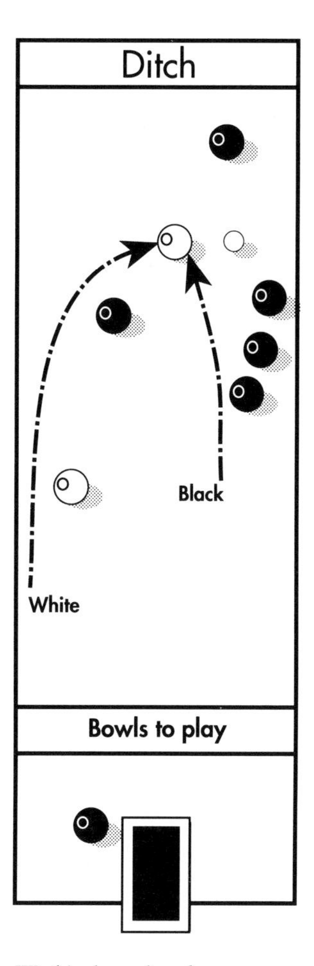

W skip has played a great 'saver' with his last bowl to draw shot, but is vulnerable to a 'take-out'. With his last bowl B skip plays a very tight shot on the forehand to remove W's shot bowl. This leaves B with a 5-count

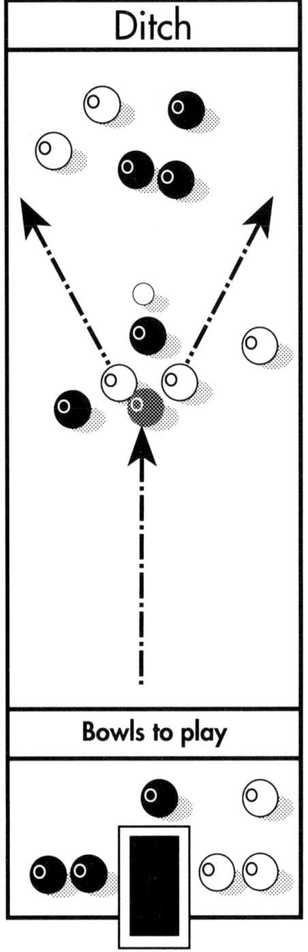

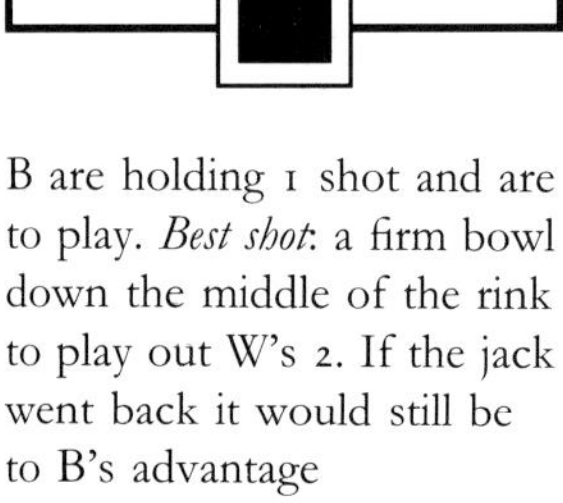

B are holding 1 shot and are to play. *Best shot*: a firm bowl down the middle of the rink to play out W's 2. If the jack went back it would still be to B's advantage

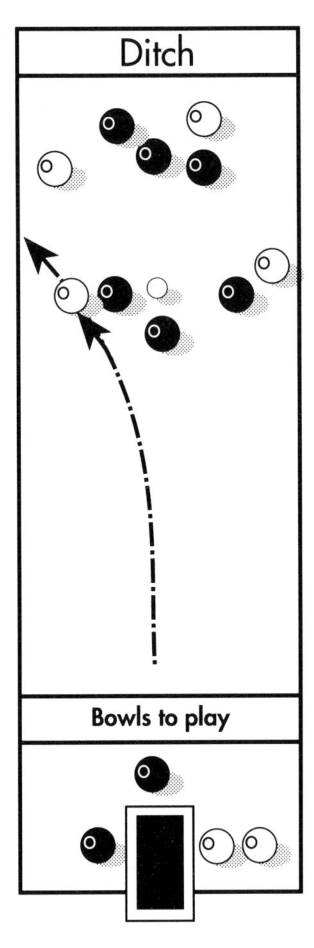

Again, B hold 1 and are to play. They could gain a much larger count by playing out W's jack-high bowl

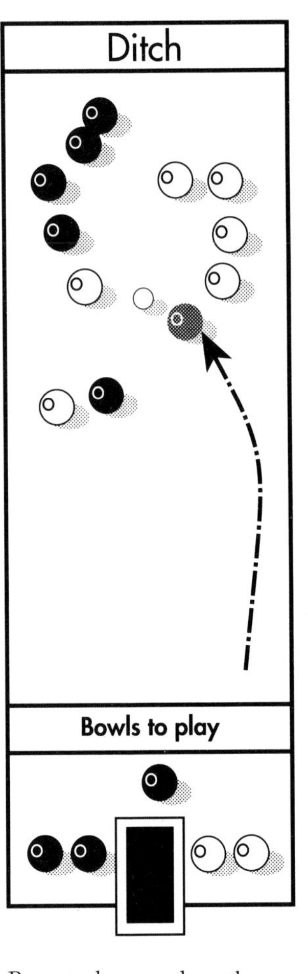

B are 2 down and to play. A forehand trail shot is risky; if it goes slightly wrong the jack may go to the right, leaving W with 4. *Best shot*: a forehand draw

The temptation to run at the jack is enormous but very risky. W is ahead by at least 4 and the head is open to a draw on the backhand. B should really be thinking about a draw to save or even to get shot. If it went just behind the jack, even better!

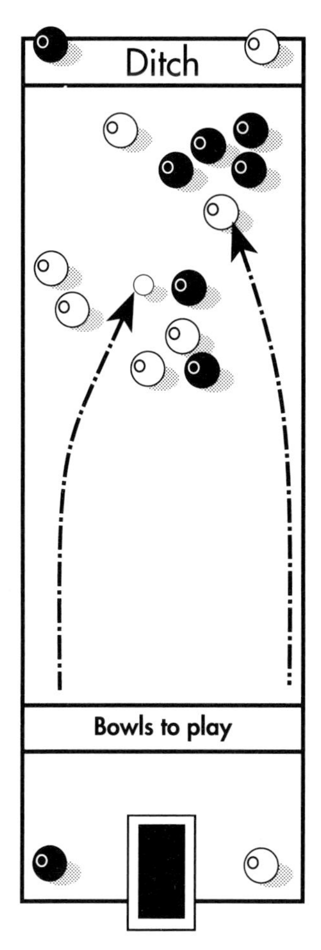

Both skips have 1 bowl left and W skip is to play. He must try to counteract the backhand trail that B might find with his last bowl. *Best shot*: an insurance shot on the forehand to finish behind the head

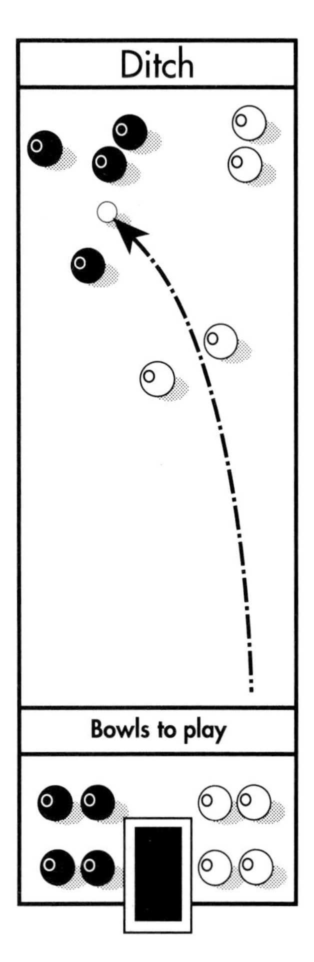

A great chance for B No. 3 to set up a potential 5-count. He should play with a yard of running to rub off W's short bowl on the right of the head and run the jack to the left. Luck is needed, but it is well worth the risk

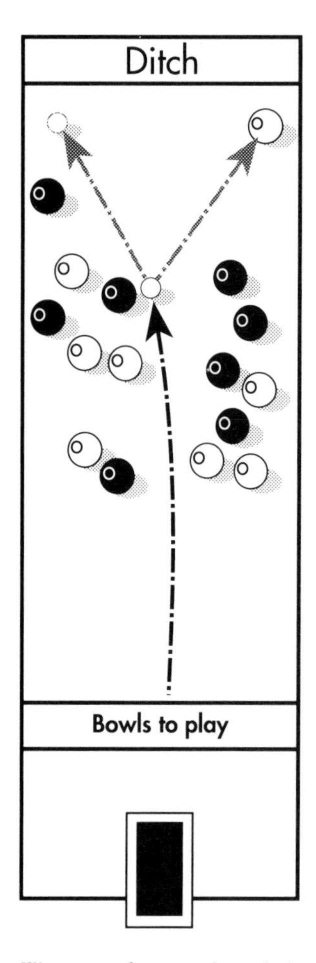

W were 1 down and needed a shot to draw to force an extra end. W skip tried to play the jack into the ditch; by gaining a 'toucher' he would have achieved his aim. However, he sliced the jack and W were still 1 down after the measure

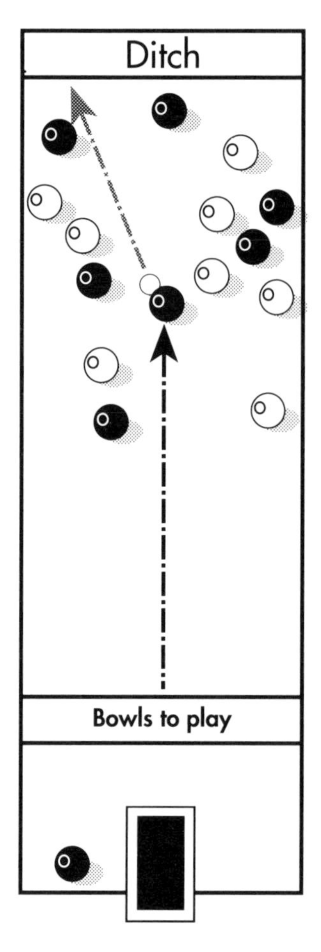

B hold 1 but need 2 to win the match. To draw a second shot would be difficult, and care must be taken not to tap shot so that the jack springs back to the waiting W bowls. *Best shot*: a shot bowl with weight on the forehand to propel the jack into the ditch

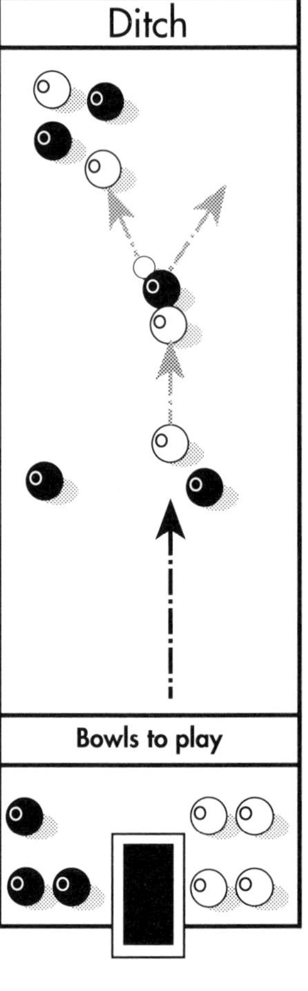

Although B hold shot, W can change that if the short front bowl is played against the second (W) bowl resting against the shot. The jack should travel back enough for the W back bowl to be shot with the B shot bowl being sent right out of the head

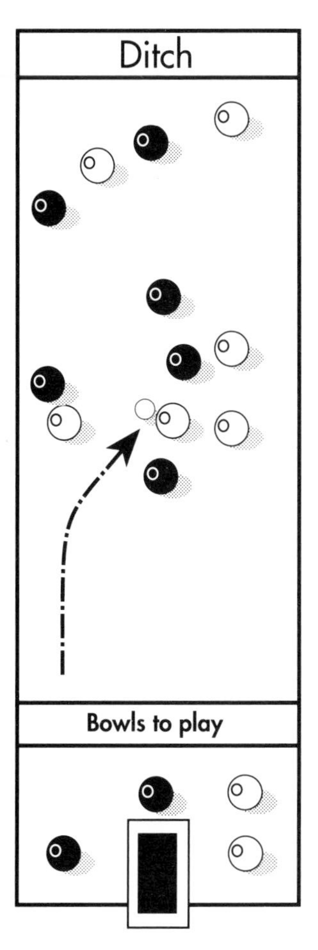

A chance for B skip to regain shot with a slightly weighted backhand draw (or wresting shot). If the jack is moved it must be in B's favour. He needs just enough weight to move W's bowl a couple of feet

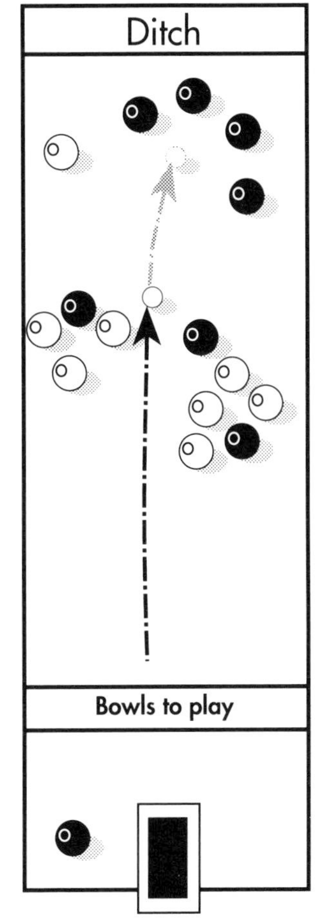

B, perhaps only 1 down (with a measure), can gain a much-needed 5 with a perfect backhand trail to run the jack 12–15 ft. In this situation little can go wrong for B

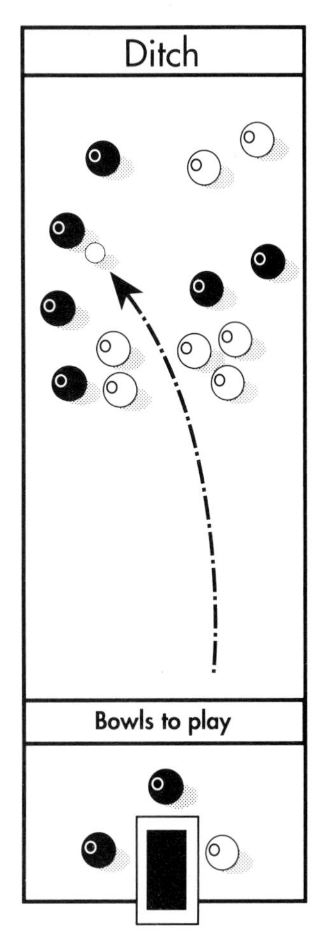

B are in a little trouble, at least 3 down. A forehand trail shot will put them back in the driving seat with 4 or 5 shots

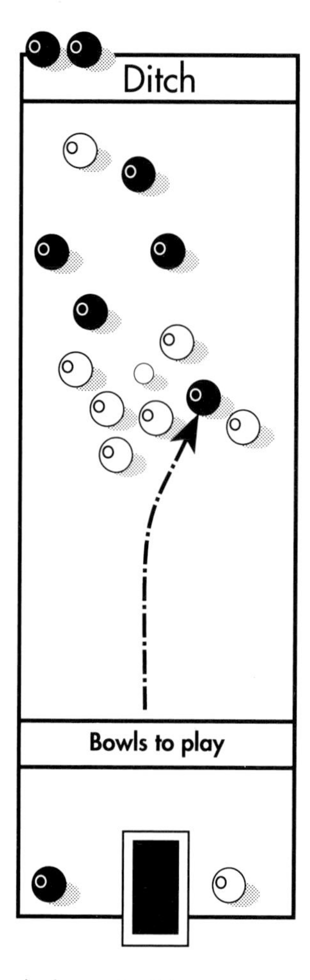

A chance for W to put pressure on the B skip, who has the last bowl. A bowl with weight on the backhand across the head will take out the B bowl in the head and give W a 5-count

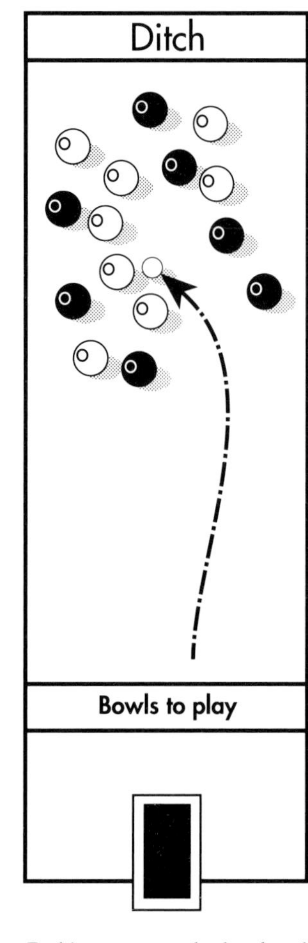

B skip must use the last bowl to play the most delicate of draw shots without moving the jack. If he does get to the jack there is a saving of at least 2 shots

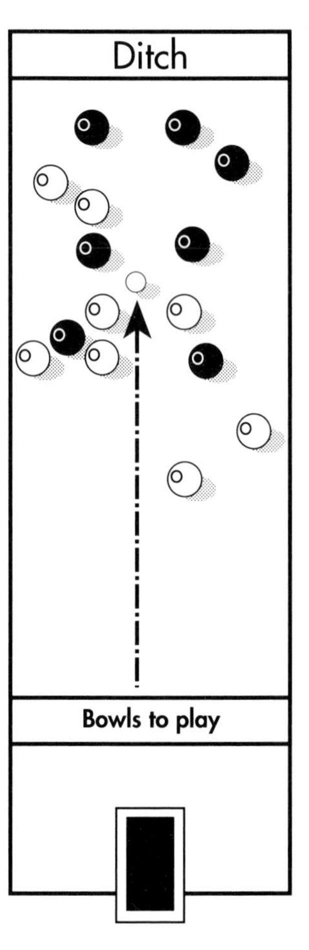

Last bowl: B skip has little option but to drive the jack into the ditch for a possible 6-shot conversion. B are 2 down but could pick up 4 with the jack and 'toucher' in the ditch

Index